T0280190

PRAISE FOR
A FAITH OF MANY ROOMS

"I have been feasting on Debie Thomas's words for years. I often say that she reads the Bible like a radiologist reads an MRI, seeing things I could never see. But in this book I get a glimpse of Debie herself, and I'm grateful. The story of her journey from the cramped closet of an evangelical childhood to the 'many rooms' of a more generous faith is one of her greatest gifts to the church, and one I hope she will continue to share. It inspires my own journey."

—**Jim Somerville**, pastor of Richmond's First Baptist Church and founder of A Sermon for Every Sunday

"For years, Debie Thomas has offered fans like me a winsome, enlightened approach to the word of God. This time, in this book, she opens the door to God's whole, colorful, many-winged house—a house where our cultures are gifts, our ancestors are prophets, everyone's story matters, and God is always near. Brilliant, carefully crafted, and heart-stopping in its beauty and honesty, this is Debie Thomas at her best."

—**Rev. Stephanie Spellers**, Canon to Presiding Bishop Michael Curry and author of *The Church Cracked Open* and *Radical Welcome*

"I found myself feeling very at home and unexpectedly exposed reading Debie Thomas's quest for a faith and a place to be at home and not an outsider. Thomas rests in Jesus's promise of a spacious, roomy Christianity that travels with us, crosses borders, and bears our sorrows. If you are curious about a faith capacious enough to embrace the entire world with reverence and humility, this story of one Malayalee woman's journey to bare her whole self to the God of the universe is a must-read. Me too, Debie—I have caught myself saying, 'Blessed Thomas (and Mary) of India, pray for us.'"

—**Winnie Varghese**, rector of St. Luke's
Episcopal Church, Atlanta, Georgia

"The Christian faith is an invitation to rest—with each other—in God's peace. Debie Thomas draws together stories about her life and from our Scriptures to help us notice a hidden truth: the here-ness of God. This book is a testimony to the Spirit's gracious care for our lives, available in every encounter with a neighbor."

—**Isaac Villegas**, Mennonite pastor and contributing
editor at *The Christian Century*

A FAITH OF MANY ROOMS

A FAITH

INHABITING A MORE

OF MANY

SPACIOUS CHRISTIANITY

ROOMS

DEBIE THOMAS

Broadleaf Books
Minneapolis

A FAITH OF MANY ROOMS
Inhabiting a More Spacious Christianity

30 29 28 27 26 25 24   2 3 4 5 6 7 8 9

Library of Congress Cataloging-in-Publication Data

Names: Thomas, Debie, author.
Title: A faith of many rooms : inhabiting a more spacious Christianity / Debie Thomas.
Description: Minneapolis, MN : Broadleaf Books, [2024]
Identifiers: LCCN 2023020604 (print) | LCCN 2023020605 (ebook) | ISBN 9781506481456 (print) | ISBN 9781506481463 (ebook)
Subjects: LCSH: Christianity. | Identification (Religion)
Classification: LCC BV4509.5 .T4845 2024 (print) | LCC BV4509.5 (ebook) | DDC 230—dc23/eng/20230831
LC record available at https://lccn.loc.gov/2023020604
LC ebook record available at https://lccn.loc.gov/2023020605

Cover design: Olga Grlic
Cover image: GettyImages-862013794

Print ISBN: 978-1-5064-8145-6
eBook ISBN: 978-1-5064-8146-3

CONTENTS

INTRODUCTION: BELONGING   1

1. A ST. THOMAS PILGRIMAGE: DOUBT   13

2. NOWHERE TO LAY HIS HEAD: LEAVING   31

3. INTO THE WILDERNESS: LOST   43

4. BEYOND BELIEF: STORY   59

5. SHE BLOWS WHERE SHE WILLS: SPIRIT   73

6. GETTING SAVED: SIN   83

7. CONSENTING TO BROKENNESS: LAMENT   105

8. BEARING GOD'S IMAGE: WOMEN   123

9. EMBRACING THE DISSONANCE: PARADOX   139

10. LIMPS AND WORMS: WRESTLING   159

CONTENTS

EPILOGUE: STAYING   173

ACKNOWLEDGMENTS   179

NOTES   181

INTRODUCTION: BELONGING

Nadhe is a treasured word in my immigrant family. It is a yearning word, shot through with nostalgia and hope. Though it has no straightforward equivalent in English, I'm always on the lookout for satisfying translations: *Birthplace. Mother country. Heart of belonging. Home.*

None of these will do. They don't capture the love, loss, and lament I hear in my family's native Malayalam. If I close my eyes, though, the South Indian word blooms in precise, Technicolor memory. An ancestral house with cool tile floors and wooden beams, surrounded by palms and mango trees. Stunningly green rice paddies in the visible distance. Coconuts so tender my grandmother could scoop out their insides like pudding. The heavy, too-sweet scent of jackfruit rotting in the sun. Sheets of water falling from the sky during the monsoon. The cool, mossy darkness of the family well, forbidden to curious children.

Though I grew up in Boston, I spent many of my childhood summers in Kerala, South India, my parents' nadhe. In the mornings, I'd take my breakfast, go sit outside on my grandparents' veranda, and stare at the clusters of children who walked past the house to school in their blue jumpers, starched blouses, and stiff pigtails. Who *were* those girls with the impossibly bright ribbons in their hair, swinging tiffin boxes on their arms? What did they think and talk and dream about? Were we the same, all of us brown-skinned kids with roots in this lush, green place? Or did the ocean that separated my everyday life from theirs signal a gulf too wide to cross?

Those schoolgirls stared right back at me. Who was I? Petite and black-haired like them, but clearly an outsider in my Kmart dresses and CVS hair clips, with my overeager smile and heavily accented Malayalam. They looked at me and giggled. They looked at me and turned away.

The experience was disorienting. Watching those girls was like gazing into an alternative mirror: the mirror that *would* have been, if my parents—by a series of circumstances so tenuous and random as to seem permanently reversible—hadn't moved to America. Like the many thousands of people who arrived in the United States in the wake of the 1965 Immigration and Naturalization Act, my parents left their beloved nadhe to make "a better life" for our family. In the early years, this meant working menial jobs—repairing shoes, sweeping floors at Macy's, chopping onions at a local French restaurant. It meant braving Boston's bitter winters in too-thin clothes. It meant scraping money together to pay for rent, groceries, car payments, babies. It meant missing India with a sadness that bordered on desperation.

Like many bicultural kids, I inherited my parents' sense of dislocation. Though my parents did, in time, make a better life for my brother and me, a life of suburban ease, comfort, and opportunity, I circled around a missing *something* for years, trying to pin it down. I was bilingual, but I felt wordless. I had friends, but I felt alone. I was American—the navy blue passports my father guarded so fiercely in his locked filing cabinet proved it—but I felt like a foreigner.

I never spoke this aloud, but at some deep level, I knew what I lacked. I lacked a world spacious enough to accommodate *all* of me: the American me, the Indian me, the fragmented me, the conflicted me.

As a child, I didn't have the language to express it, but what I hungered for was coherence. Space. Belonging. Nadhe. A home where my inner and outer lives could align.

———

For many people, the search for a spiritual nadhe has been no less complicated than my search for a cultural one. Churchgoing, which used to be a mainstay of American culture, is increasingly an oddity. Christian affiliation is on the wane across all demographics and denominations in the United States. Increasing numbers of people, especially young people, are leaving the faith and not coming back. Meanwhile, the ranks of Americans who describe their religious identity as atheist, agnostic, or "nothing in particular," are steadily rising. According to a 2022 Pew Research Center report, if these trends continue, Christians could make up less than half of the US population within a few decades, with religious "nones" representing as much as 52 percent of the population by 2070.

The reasons for this exodus are many, and we'll look at some of them in this book. But the consequential fact is that the religious landscape of the country is changing. Christianity is no longer America's cultural default, and its future—for better or for worse—is up for grabs. Finding a viable way forward in this context requires a courageous willingness to reexamine and re-*vision* the religion of our pasts.

At a more personal level, all of us must reckon with the faith—or lack of faith—we've inherited from the generations that came before us. I am the daughter, granddaughter, and daughter-in-law of evangelical Christian pastors who trace their indigenous religious roots back to the first century CE (the historical period following Jesus's birth). As my father so often preached on Sunday mornings, we count ourselves among the "original" Christians: direct heirs of Jesus's disciple Thomas, who we believe brought the gospel to India. Ours is a heritage that long predates the ascendancy of Christianity in the West, and the weight of that tradition is both hefty and formidable.

The weight of translating faith across countries, cultures, and languages is heavy as well. Until I left home for college in the early 1990s, I spent every Sunday morning in a large, multiethnic evangelical church in downtown Boston, where my father served as an associate minister. This was the church that paid our bills, that made possible our "better" American lives. There, as is the case with many Christians in the United States, especially those in majority white and sometimes multiethnic congregations, the God we worshipped was unabashedly white and male. His Caucasian angels adorned the organ in fading oils and watercolors, and his blue-eyed apostles lined the upper balcony in stained glass. This God appreciated pipe organs, choir robes, Easter processions, and potlucks abounding in chicken casseroles.

In his white American guise, God was like Pa from *Little House on the Prairie*, Mike from *The Brady Bunch*, and Father March from *Little Women* all rolled up together. He spoke English in the

New International Version, ate honey-dipped donuts during coffee hour, and shared Hershey's Kisses out of his suit pockets in the narthex.

On Sunday afternoons, though, my family left white God behind and headed to another house of faith—a house closer to my family's nadhe. My father named this makeshift church the Kerala Christian Fellowship and pastored it for well over a decade—not for pay, but for the consolations of familiarity, kinship, and belonging. The immigrant Indian families who attended those 4:00 p.m. services preferred to worship in our mother tongue, Malayalam, and to practice a form of Christianity more in keeping with the traditional South Asian forms they missed so deeply.

In "Indian church," as we called it, the women and girls sat apart from the men and boys. We dressed in modest Indian garb, covered our heads, and shunned the decadence of makeup, jewelry, written prayers, candles, incense, icons, and visual representations of God. Whereas American church was ornate and scripted, Indian church was informal and lively. We clapped our hands, smacked our tambourines, and sang haunting hymns of exile, loss, separation, and homecoming. Worshippers prophesied and spoke in tongues, and my father's sermons lauded the virtues of Indian culture as often as they did the importance of holy living.

The God we worshipped in Indian church was male and colorless. I never envisioned him as brown, as I had no models for a God who looked like me in our strictly iconoclastic church services. But he was fluent in Malayalam, and he preferred charismatic worship. The heavenly realm he lived in looked a lot like the tropical South Asian paradise my parents missed so keenly.

Like every good Protestant minister, my father preached grace in that Indian church. It was grace we stood in, grace that saved, grace that kept us all from hell and wrath and damnation. But grace in its unpredictable wildness couldn't sit well with the dictates of a religion that prized authority, conformity, and submission above all things—especially for women. Neither could it find an entirely hospitable home in the honor-shame culture of our community, a culture in which every person's actions reverberated like earthquakes across a small, shared landscape. In the "glass house" in which I lived as a preacher's daughter, my job was to honor God with my quietness, my self-denial, and my unquestioning obedience.

There is much to love about the faith tradition I come from. To this day, I'm grateful to evangelicalism, in both of the cultural guises it took for me, for shaping my deepest loves, hopes, desires, and priorities. If I learned anything growing up, it is that the spiritual life *matters*, and matters profoundly. *Casual, optional, complacent, tangential*: these aren't words I associate with faith, because I grew up surrounded by people who took discipleship seriously. From them, I learned to focus a good portion of my time and attention on the big questions: Who am I? What is my purpose? Who is God? What is "the Good"? How should I live? I was still a little girl when I learned to prioritize these matters. It was a good way to grow up.

I'm also grateful to my childhood churches for steeping me in Scripture. As soon as I was old enough to read, I learned that God's Word is worth reading—not just for scholars and preachers but for everyone. Because of that early literacy, I still recognize the Bible as a treasure trove, a book to take seriously for its wisdom, truthfulness, complexity, and beauty.

By extension, I also know that words—poems, letters, proverbs, stories—matter to God. After all, "in the beginning was the Word" (John 1:1). *Logos.* Narrative. Story. Speech. I love that God communicates through words in myriad and surprising ways, and that God delights in me when I use my own words to communicate back.

And I'm thankful that my earliest faith communities introduced me to a God who is personal. Not all faith traditions, even Christian ones, highlight the relational, the experiential, and the intimate when they describe the Divine. It was no small thing for me to learn early on that the Creator of the universe is not an abstraction, an idea, a politics, or a worldview—that the Creator is a person who knows me and loves me.

Of course, the irony is that the same rigorous faith tradition that formed me also taught me a healthy skepticism toward *all* traditions. I was taught that our work as Christians is to ask, seek, and knock, that we need to *keep* asking hard questions, "testing the spirits" (1 John 4:1), and pursuing the good and the true, even if that pursuit leads us into strange territory. I'm grateful that I learned early on not to take faith for granted. But no one (least of all I) knew that I'd eventually turn these critical tools against my own tradition. Regardless, the tools were right there all along.

I lived in the glass house and straddled my two expressions of evangelicalism as faithfully as I could for a long time—trying, like Alice in Wonderland, to cram my alarmingly growing self into an ever-shrinking space. But my doubts, fears, and objections kept spilling out through the doors and windows, refusing to accept confinement. Eventually, I couldn't fit myself inside the house of evangelical Christian faith at all. The walls crumbled, and all I could see around me were its ruins.

The ruins were both theological and personal. I'd been raised to live in a world where the Bible was not only inerrant but also straightforwardly sufficient for all my hardest questions about reality. I'd been prepared for a world that ran on unshakable creeds and doctrines: as long as I believed the right things, the earth would turn, and everything that mattered in my life would be well. I'd been taught to shun doubt as a diabolical enemy of faith—an insidious force bent on my destruction. I'd been raised for a world in which God's activity is beautifully self-evident; direct and discernible answers to prayer are my spiritual birthright; and perpetual hope, healing, certainty, and joy constitute the norms of the Christian life. When that world turned out to be false, I became unhoused. Homeless. I felt like I'd never find nadhe again.

Christian Scripture is rife with metaphors of roominess. Yet the language I hear from people struggling in their faith lives is the language of narrowness, constriction, and confinement. "Christianity is too small to hold my story," people tell me in my work as a minister and writer. Or: "Christianity is too culturally and historically particular." "Christianity is white, macho, racist, and colonialist." "Christianity is inhospitable to diversity and difference." "Christianity requires me to check my brain at the door." "Christianity's claims don't align with my lived experience."

As more and more people leave Christianity because of its oppressive smallness, our collective trauma deepens. Both the church and those who feel they have no choice but to abandon it face loss, bewilderment, and grief. Walter Brueggemann describes the experience this way: "The world for which you have been so carefully prepared is being taken away from you, by the grace of God."

That grace isn't always obvious when we're forced to leave the known and the familiar. Often it feels impossible to take hold of God's care when we're stumbling through the ruins of what used to be home. It takes time, patience, and the help of a discerning spiritual community to notice grace in the rubble.

We often don't know what gives us ballast until it disappears. We can't see what we're made of until we're unmade. We think we're safe in our sturdy, comfortable homes of faith—and then the ground begins to shake. The earth heaves, our feet slip, and we grab wildly in all directions at once: backward, forward, sideways, down. Where is safety? What is real? Where can we go? To whom do we belong?

"Disillusionment is, literally, the loss of an illusion—about ourselves, about the world, about God," writes Barbara Brown Taylor in *God in Pain*. "And while it is almost always a painful thing, it is never a bad thing to lose the lies we have mistaken for the truth."

For many, the slow, messy process of "losing the lies" as a Christian involves loss and pain, yes. But it can also lead us to discover a spaciousness at the heart of Christianity that we hadn't known existed.

In the Gospel of John, Jesus describes the kingdom of God as a house of "many rooms" (14:2, NIV). Growing up, I was taught that Jesus's claim applied literally and exclusively to the afterlife. To heaven. But insofar as Jesus also said that the kingdom of God is *within and among us, here and now,* I have come to see a much wider application for this beautiful architectural metaphor.

If Jesus delights in preparing "many rooms" for us, it means that the realm of God is by nature wide, abundant, and capacious. Where God dwells—and where we dwell *with* God—there is expansiveness. Where God reigns, there is generosity, variety, and plenitude. Space to wander. Space to explore. Space to find, lose, and find again. With their hidden corners, nooks, and crannies, each room beckons us with a warm and gentle hospitality.

In the chapters that follow, we will explore these "many rooms." Both Scripture and my experiences as a bicultural woman living in America have opened them up to me. I want to share how my spiritual house has expanded into a place where I no longer have to compartmentalize my life into separate, isolated realms: My intellect. My race. My gender. My feminism. My culture. My ethnicity. I want to describe what nadhe looks like for me now and to explore the grace of God that suffuses its many rooms.

Your nadhe will likely look different from mine. The rooms in which God meets, hosts, and nourishes you will be unique to your own spiritual journey. But the same grace permeates them all.

Most of all, I want to suggest that God is just as graced by the possibility of spaciousness as we are. For years, I assumed that the only person suffering within my cramped Christianity was me. But now I wonder if God, too, feels caged in by our tiny, closet-sized faith lives. What if the religious worlds for which we were so carefully prepared limit God as much as they limit us? Maybe God is asking for room, too—room to exist in our lives in God's full, multifaceted complexity.

If God shares the same hunger for spaciousness that has driven me for so many years, perhaps my core desire for nadhe has been a magnet, pulling me closer and closer to God's own heart. If so, then when we move into God's roomy house, we will finally become the hosts of homes hospitable for God. Homes spacious enough to welcome God as God is.

———

Those childhood trips to India always began with a tiring journey. After our long, transatlantic flight from Boston to Mumbai, we'd crawl our way through a bewildering and chaotic customs line, only to board another plane to Kerala. Then came a long taxi ride, in a dusty Ambassador crammed full of our suitcases. Finally my parents, brother, and I would take a rattling autorickshaw into my grandparents' little village. By then, we'd be sweaty, hungry, and exhausted.

The village didn't have reliable electricity, so we'd hazard the winding dirt roads in pitch darkness, our eyes hungry for a first glimpse of the family house. We'd peer and strain, looking, looking. Finally, we'd turn a corner—and there my grandmother would be, standing in the courtyard in her white sari, a tall candle burning in her hands. How long she'd stood there, waiting for us, we never knew.

She'd usher us in, caress our faces, and hold us tight. For her, the whole enterprise was a miracle and joy. The foreign country we'd just returned from. The gigantic plane—*chairs in the sky?*—that carried us from one side of the world to another. The impossible ocean crossing.

The first words I'd hear her breathe were always the same. First, "Praise God." And second, "Welcome home."

My grandmother died a few years ago, at the age of one hundred. But whenever I remember her, it is God I imagine.

The God of my nadhe. The God of the many rooms. She's the patient, unwearying grandmother, cutting the darkness with her fragile, steady light. She knows that there's no homecoming without a journey, and she knows that the journey is risky, tiring, treacherous. She knows how to offer refuge at journey's end.

"Come in and sit down," she tells me, her soft fingers wrapped around my arm. The candlelight flickers. I step inside. "You've traveled a long way," she says, cupping my face in her hands. I relax into her touch, knowing I am seen, held, known. At journey's end is unconditional love. "You can rest now. *Rest.* You're home."

1 | A ST. THOMAS PILGRIMAGE: DOUBT

It's July in Kerala, and we need a break from the heat. I stick my face out of the car window and watch as the lush coconut groves and banana trees of the south give way to the tea plantations and foggy foothills of the northern mountains. A family friend has suggested this day trip to the cool mountainous region of Vagamon, a three-hour drive from my father's ancestral home. As the temperature drops, I send her a whispered thank you and glance at my husband and children, hoping the change is giving them respite. Poor kids; the heat has ravished them. It looks as if chicken pox, eczema, and premature acne have waged wars across their faces.

It is 2008, and we are in India for a three-week vacation that is turning into a pilgrimage, a search for my religious roots. Back in my American life, I'm a graduate student in creative writing, trying to sort out my thesis. I want to write about my faith, but I don't know how. My faith is in crisis, and I'm afraid. So I've decided to begin at the beginning. To return to the ancient place that birthed my relationship with God.

Our driver winds his way around hairpin turns and alarming cutbacks for a few more miles, and the scenery startles me again and again. The tourist brochures call Kerala "God's own country," and today, I understand why. It's monsoon season, and the landscape is blanketed in an almost fluorescent green, every inch of the place riotously colorful, fecund, lush, *alive.* I want to revel in it. I don't want to miss even a moment of its wild, thriving beauty.

I see the sign first, and point to it as our driver slows down. *Kurismala Ashram*: "The Hill of the Cross." Under that, in small block print, the name we're looking for: "The Mount of St. Thomas."

After a friendly exchange with a monk at the gates of the monastery, we drive past a church and some modest living quarters, following an unpaved road until it ends in a wide, grassy valley. We park and pile out slowly, stiff and uncoordinated after the long drive. A wet, cold wind slaps at my face, more astonishing than troublesome.

My daughter plants herself in front of a large billboard to the left of the car and demands a translation. This is not a tourist site, the billboard explains in Malayalam, but a sacred place for reflection, worship, and prayer. Warnings against graffiti and litter follow. "The cows haven't read the sign," my son says gleefully, jumping over piles of manure in the scraggly grass.

Fog obscures the hills, settling, dissipating, and settling again. My family scatters in different directions across the bowl-shaped valley, stretching achy limbs, taking photographs, shivering. I walk into every patch of fog that hinders my view, enticed by bits of bright, improbable color in the grayness. Statues. The hills rising in every direction are dotted with colorful, painted statues.

To my right at a distance, Christ kneels among a cluster of mossy rocks, his dark head bowed in prayer. Across the valley another Christ figure hovers over a huge blue and green globe, his feet grazing the Arctic Circle, his arms outstretched to embrace invisible stars. Squinting against the fine drizzle in the air now, I see the disciples. Peter, Andrew, Thaddeus, James. They sit, kneel, stand, and recline, eleven of them winding their holy way up the hills to a life-size crucifixion scene far above the valley.

But the disciple I've crossed the Atlantic to see, the patron saint of Indian Christianity, is not among the eleven. He is on a hill of his own, raised atop a pedestal one hundred and twenty stone steps above the ground. As I start climbing, I gasp at how huge he is. Even with his face shrouded in fog, he rules the valley.

At the base of his statue, the doubting disciple's famous confession stands out in crisp black font: "My Lord and my God" (John 20:28). Thomas wears a light blue cloak over a white tunic and holds a black Bible in his left hand. In his right he grips what is either a staff or a spear, and his forefinger, a witness to the world, is covered in blood. His face is bearded and angular. Behind him, an austere cross leans against a stone, a stark reminder that he would suffer a martyr's death.

It's an impressive representation of Thomas, but it's not the grandest one I've seen on my trip. At Palayur, the oldest church in India, I've seen the apostle set in gleaming silver atop the roof, alongside life-size granite statues depicting scenes of his life and ministry. At Niranam, the church where he is believed to have lived during his stay in Kerala, I've seen him carved in rich, reddish wood, adorned with marigolds and painted in vivid color as an Indian man, with skin as brown and hair as curly black as my own.

In contrast, this statue on the hill is weather-worn, splintered, faded, mundane. There's no reason to linger; it's starting to rain in earnest, and I know that the kids are hungry. But I can't quite leave. I sit down in the wet grass instead, so that the statue looms even larger.

The expression on Thomas's face is serene, wholly unlike what it must have been two thousand years ago, when he returned to the house where he and his fellow disciples were hiding after Jesus's death. That day, when his friends told him that their beloved Jesus was alive, Thomas refused to believe them. The expression on his face must have been incredulous. Alarmed. Perhaps even furious.

Thomas gets a bad rap in American Christianity. He's "Doubting Thomas": the cynic, the unbeliever, the skeptic, the holdout. His reluctance to accept the testimony of his fellow disciples, his insistence on physical proof of Jesus's resurrection, his late arrival to the faith of his peers—these are often described as spiritual flaws. As signs of stubbornness, or of a weak commitment to God.

To be honest, Thomas wasn't a biblical character I admired as a little girl and young adult. Deeply rooted in a faith that left no room for mistakes and missteps, I didn't know what to do with Doubting Thomas, except to look down on him.

He was everything I wanted *not* to be. He was everything I was *instructed* not to be. Cautious. Skeptical. Stubborn. Daring.

These days, however, I wonder if Thomas represents the *best* we might become, because spiritual weakness is no longer what I see when I look at him. I see a man who yearned for a living encounter with Jesus—an encounter *of his own*, unmediated by the claims and assumptions of others. A man who wouldn't settle for hand-me-down religion but demanded a firsthand experience of God to anchor and enliven his faith. To me, this speaks not only to Thomas's integrity but to his hunger. His desire. His investment. He wasn't spiritually passive. He didn't want the outer trappings of religion if he couldn't know its fiery core. He was alive with longing.

According to John's Gospel, Thomas had to wait in suspense and uncertainty for a whole week after his friends first told him they'd seen Jesus. What, I wonder, did that week feel like for the disciple who missed Jesus the first time around? Did he pity his fellow disciples for what must have struck him as their grief-stricken delusions? Or did he fear (as I so often do) that he'd missed the memo, missed the boat, missed the glory? That the risen Jesus had passed him by? That he was destined only ever to know God secondhand?

In *Inspired: Slaying Giants, Walking on Water, and Loving the Bible Again*, Rachel Held Evans writes about the power of origin stories to make and unmake meaning, to tell us who we are and why our existence matters, especially in moments of loss or crisis. "Origin stories are rarely straightforward history," she writes. "Over the years, they morph into a colorful amalgam of truth and myth, nostalgia and cautionary tale, the shades of their significance brought out by the particular light of a particular moment."

In the faith community that raised me, the fact that St. Thomas came to India and shared the gospel with our ancestors holds all kinds of significance. I can't count the number of times I've heard my father tell the story. When he tells it to people who are not Indian, his telling is proud and almost defiant: "We are *not* converts. We *didn't* come to faith through white missionaries. Our Christian heritage goes further back than yours."

Even as a little girl, I understood that casting Westerners as the Johnny-come-latelies to Christianity had a powerful leveling effect. A *vindicating* effect. My immigrant elders needed the reordering of hierarchies that "The Apostle of India" demands of white Christians. The story isn't simply about equality. It's about a superiority born of blood, tradition, lineage, and history.

The story carries a different inflection when my elders tell it to non-Christian *Indians*. In those conversations, they wish to indigenize Jesus—to make his story one of India's own, such that he becomes no less authentically South Asian than Hinduism, Sikhism, Jainism, or Islam. Given India's British colonial history, this claim of deep origins—of cultural purity, fidelity, and indigeneity—works to counter the claim that Indian Christians are simply whitewashed and colonized.

Rachel Held Evans argues that our spiritual growth as Christians begins with an honest and critical look at our origin stories. Neither an enshrinement of them, nor a wholesale rejection, but a willingness to engage the stories at their best *and* their worst: "Spiritual maturation requires untangling these stories, sorting fact from fiction (or, more precisely, truth from untruth), and embracing those stories that move us toward wholeness while rejecting or reinterpreting those that do harm."

On that windy afternoon in Kerala, sitting on the Mount of St. Thomas, I wanted to make his story my own. To make it big enough and flexible enough to fit me: my ambivalence about tradition, my unease with Scripture, my uncertainty about my Indianness. I didn't want to deploy my origins to prove my own spiritual purity or disprove anyone else's. I didn't want to endorse a narrative that was about insiders and outsiders, authentic Christians and inauthentic ones. Most of all, I didn't want to bind myself to a heritage frozen in time—a two-thousand-year-old heritage that prohibits movement, evolution, confusion, and creativity.

I'm learning to return to the story on my own terms, looking for gaps, looking for nooks and crannies, looking for flexibility. I'm not afraid of messiness; I crave it. If there's room for messiness, there's room for me.

The Indian legend of St. Thomas is not a single legend but a vast collection of stories spanning centuries. I started exploring them in 2008, and I haven't stopped since.

One of the most basic, pared-down versions, preserved by village *asharis* (bards) in a rich oral tradition of songs, ballads, and dances, goes like this:

Thomas sailed to Kerala in 52 CE, intending to preach to the Jewish colonies settled near Cochin. After making both Jewish and Brahmin converts there, he followed the coastline south, winning hundreds of followers in the villages of my ancestors. After establishing *ezharappallikal* (seven churches) along the waterways of Kerala, he crossed the subcontinent to Mylapore, on the East Coast near Madras.

There his preaching and proselytizing successes aroused the jealousy and hostility of devout Brahmins, who speared him to death in 72 CE. The martyr's relics stayed in Mylapore until 232 CE, when an Indian king carried them to Edessa, a city in modern-day Turkey. In 1258, the relics were taken to Italy, where they remain to this day. South Indian Christians, however, still venerate Mylapore as the apostle's official resting place, and many hundreds make pilgrimages to his death site each year.

That's one version of the story. Others are more colorful, mystical, and even absurd. There's no way to verify any of them, of course, but they tug at me anyway. Something in me wants to know who this disciple was, this bold doubter who left the only home he knew to walk where my ancestors walked and live where my ancestors lived, sowing the seeds of faith that are still flowering in me.

If nothing else, I want to connect the dots of his Indian life so that I can connect my own. What does it mean to love Jesus in strange places and new languages? What does it mean to find God among people you never expected to make your own? What does it mean to trust a story so completely that you *must* share it—even if the sharing puts your very life at risk?

According to *The Acts of Thomas*, an apocryphal text dating from the middle of the third century, the eleven disciples gathered in the upper room after Jesus's ascension, to discuss how they would carry out the great commission (Jesus's command that they go into all the world and preach the gospel). Eventually, they cast lots to determine where each person would go. India fell to Thomas, but he refused. "Anywhere but India," he said.

He had his reasons, I'm sure, and I have to admit that they were likely compelling ones: It would be too difficult to communicate across language and culture barriers. How would he remain kosher in a foreign land? What if the mission was an embarrassing failure?

Ever the curmudgeon and the skeptic, Thomas persisted in his refusal even after Christ himself appeared to him in a dream and told him to take courage and go.

Meanwhile, according to various oral traditions, a North Indian king named Gundaphores sent a merchant to Jerusalem, with instructions to bring back a skilled carpenter who could build him a magnificent palace. The merchant, directed by Christ, landed right on Thomas's doorstep. After a great deal more grumbling and lots of divine intervention, the doubting disciple made his reluctant way to India. There Gundaphores commissioned him to build the palace, gave him a large sum of money from the royal treasury, and set him a deadline.

I'm guessing Thomas *wanted* to honor his contract with this powerful king. Maybe he started out earnestly, choosing materials, honing his craft, and finding a comforting kinship with Jesus, the carpenter's son, as he put his mind and his hands to work.

But then his heart stopped him. When he saw the poverty, oppression, and suffering of the people in Gundaphores's kingdom, he was grieved and outraged, and he decided that he couldn't spend money on an opulent palace that would be surrounded by the penniless and destitute. So instead, he gave the king's money away to the poor.

When the king returned at the appointed time and found his palace unbuilt, he flew into a rage. But, according to the text, Thomas was unfazed. He calmly insisted that he *had* built a palace for Gundaphores, a particularly lavish one that the king would see upon his death. Needless to say, this reassurance didn't stop the furious king from throwing Thomas into prison and scheduling his execution.

Right around this time, the king's brother Gad fell ill and died. As Gad entered heaven, the angels invited him to walk freely among the celestial mansions and choose one for himself. But when Gad pointed out his favorite mansion, the angels shook their heads. That one, they said, was reserved for Gad's royal

21

brother, Gundaphores. It had been specially built by Thomas—
"that Christian" in India.

In the predictably redemptive climax of the story, Gad
received divine permission to return to earth and tell Gundaphores the news that he had a gorgeous heavenly mansion waiting for him—a mansion Thomas had built by loving and laboring
among the least of God's children.

The astonished Gundaphores accepted Christ as Savior on
the spot, and Thomas, freed from prison, baptized both broth-
ers on the same day. After breaking bread and taking wine with
them, Thomas left Gundaphores's kingdom to win many more
converts across South India.

I love this story. I love what it suggests about the gospel's
power to open us up to wider and *wilder* possibilities of love. Not
just love for the familiar, but love for the stranger, the outcast, the
unorthodox, the other.

The story begins with Thomas resisting God's call with every
excuse he can think of. He doesn't want to go to India. He doesn't
want to compromise his religious purity by eating, living, and
ministering with foreigners. He doesn't want to do the hard work
it takes to bridge the barriers of language, culture, and tradition
that make Jesus's radical practice of love so challenging. After all,
this is the Thomas who held himself back when his friends first
embraced the resurrection. He's not one to take bold leaps.

And yet. Thomas has also spent years watching Jesus embrace
the leper, feed the beggar, honor the sex worker, and elevate the
stranger. He heard Jesus predict his death and responded fatalis-
tically by saying what everyone else is afraid to say: "Let's go to
Jerusalem and die with him" (John 11:16). He knows firsthand
that great love resides in broken, wounded bodies.

So he goes to India despite his many reservations, and allows his heart to be broken open by people who are utterly unlike him. He makes room, and faith is born.

———————

Some variations on the Thomas story claim that the doubting disciple met the magi on his way to India and baptized those famed wise ones himself. *The Passing of Mary*, an apocryphal text attributed to Joseph of Arimathea, claims that Thomas was miraculously transported from India back to Jerusalem to witness Mary's assumption into heaven.

Other accounts describe miraculous healings, exorcisms, and ecstatic visions. Some suggest that Thomas was killed for refusing to worship an image of Kali, a goddess of Hindu mythology. Some sources even credit the dust in Thomas's grave with potent healing powers. St. Ephrem, a devotional hymn writer of the fourth century, quoted the devil himself speaking in awe of Thomas as "the Apostle I slew in India." According to oral tradition, some Christian communities in South India teach that the apostle literally lives among them as a patron saint, healer, and protector to this very day.

I know that Thomas's Indian sojourns are unprovable. The earliest documented allusions to Thomas's presence in India hail from the third and fourth centuries, leaving a two-hundred-year gap in the historical record that many scholars find troubling. We also don't know for sure what the early church fathers were referring to when they mentioned "India." They might have meant Ethiopia, Afghanistan, Persia, or even China when they named the subcontinent in their writings.

On the other hand, archaeologists have established that King Gundaphores was, in fact, a historical character. Dated coins bearing his name and image suggest that he enjoyed a long reign in India during the middle of the first century. We know, too, that the spice trade thrived under the reign of Caesar Augustus, and that the trick of sailing with the monsoon was likely discovered in the first century. Roman trading vessels made frequent trips to the bazaars of South India during Thomas's lifetime.

So if the apostle had wanted to reach the subcontinent, he could have boarded a ship quite easily. In fact, his journey across the Red Sea would have taken just under forty days.

———

What would have happened to Thomas, I wonder, if his friends had shunned him for his inconvenient doubts after the resurrection? If they'd reacted to his skepticism with fear, as if it were potentially contagious? What if they'd staged an intervention? Sat him down, read him proof texts, and prayed over him until he caved?

As far as we know, Thomas's fellow disciples allowed him to wrestle with the possibility of resurrection for as long as he needed to. They didn't kick him out of the upper room. They didn't pressure him to accept their testimony. They didn't mock, belittle, or isolate him. Instead, they held space for him. Made room for him. They offered him a radical kind of welcome: the permission to stick around as he was, full of ambivalence and doubt in the midst of their joy.

How different churches would be if they embraced the reality of doubt as generously as Jesus and his other disciples embraced Thomas. The disciples allowed him to voice both his skepticism and his yearning to see the risen Jesus with his own eyes. Though they freely shared their testimonies with him, they simultaneously gave him time and space to encounter Jesus on his own.

I can't help but believe that Thomas's doubts served him well in the end. After all, *something* emboldened him to carry the story of Jesus into the land of my ancestors. Something allowed him to die for the very faith he initially couldn't muster, even among friends. That *something* began with a bold insistence on a divine encounter of his own. The Jesus whose good news Thomas gave his life to share was a Messiah he had waited for. A teacher and friend who loved him in his doubt, and who tested, tried, humbled, and finally empowered him.

The story of Thomas in Scripture reassures me that the journey of faith can be slow and winding. Thomas dared to confess uncertainty in the midst of those who were certain. He recognized his Lord in wounds, scars, hurts, and raw places—not in cleanness, neatness, perfection, or glory. In the end, he embraced faith because the house of God was roomy enough for his doubts.

But in case we're tempted to see the journey from doubt to faith as a one-time-only deal, Thomas has more to teach us. Even after his encounter with Jesus, his faith had to change and expand. In the Indian tradition that extends beyond the canonical Scriptures, I see a disciple who feared to leave the safety of the upper room—the small Christianity he started out with—even when Jesus asked him to. Thomas was a disciple who took his time getting brave and heading out, who had to choose faith and courage not once, but over and over again.

Thomas headed to India because he finally decided that he was the heir of a story too big to tame or confine, a story that *had* to venture into strange, unfamiliar territory and become what it would become. He was a man who learned to love a people he initially feared would alienate and contaminate him. He took literally the "many rooms" of Jesus's teaching and built celestial mansions out of pity, mercy, and compassion. He became a man who willingly died for a truth he started out doubting.

I went in search of Thomas all those years ago because I wanted to see the fruits of a life lived in honest acceptance of doubt and complexity. I wanted to experience how God can still bless and multiply the witness of a disciple who struggled to trust, who yearned for God but found the path of faith rocky, lonely, and hard. Because isn't this all of us, at least some of the time? Don't we all wrestle with hidden doubts, hidden fears, relentless questions? Don't we all wonder sometimes if the resurrection will pass us by?

We live in an age of deep skepticism. Easy, clear answers to the Big Questions—Who are we? What does it mean to live a good life? Why are we here? Where are we headed? What is our purpose?—arouse suspicion, not admiration. In this context, I wonder if our willingness to give a more honest accounting of the Christian faith, an accounting that names the ongoing reality of doubt in our lives, will make for a more credible and durable witness. What if doubt itself can be testimony?

If nothing else, the apostle Thomas assures me that the business of the good news—of accepting it, of living it out, and of sharing it with the world—is tough. It's okay to waver. It's okay to take our time. It's okay to probe, prod, and insist on more. Whatever "really happened" two thousand years ago in the life of this complicated disciple, I am grateful that our tradition chose to preserve his stories. I am grateful that my family's nadhe figures in these stories.

I no longer need Thomas to authenticate, indigenize, or legitimize my faith. I need Thomas—doubter and disciple, agnostic and apostle—to show me what faith truly is.

———

Like most spiritual searches, my St. Thomas pilgrimage to India doesn't happen in a vacuum. Kerala, my birthplace, has changed dramatically since my childhood. Every house I visit boasts of children and grandchildren who have grown up and gone away to America, Europe, or the Middle East, leaving a lone grandmother, uncle, or sister behind. Some houses are locked up completely, overgrown and empty. Others are falling apart, with no one left nearby to maintain them. Land that used to be richly cultivated lies fallow for lack of workers. All of this angers me, though I know my anger is unfair. Who, among the thousands of immigrants who left Kerala in the 1950s and '60s, flinging themselves to New York, Texas, Germany, England, Dubai, could have imagined what they were doing to the place they left behind? They believed Kerala would be there for them always, waiting, patient, unchanging. Eager to embrace them with open arms when they returned. But the people who would have offered that embrace are gone now. Many, like my grandparents, have passed away. Many, like my parents, have made new lives abroad. The old roots remain only in memory.

If my children visit Kerala someday, they will find themselves little more than tourists. They'll sleep in hotels and eat in restaurants. They'll walk past rubber plantations, coconut groves, farmland, and forest that might have belonged to their ancestors, but they will experience those landscapes as outsiders. As strangers.

I want to pretend this isn't true. I want to pretend that time, airplanes, green cards, and passports don't matter. I want to press a talismanic mantra into my own ears, and theirs: "You're from somewhere. This is your land, your people, your history, your home. You're not without tradition. You're not homeless. *You belong.*"

At nine and six years old, the kids are too young to care. But *I* care. Sitting at St. Thomas's feet, I tell myself I will pummel this place and this religion into a home if it's the last thing I do. Maybe this is what the legend of the apostle is for. Maybe this is why I've come.

I look up at the statue again, wishing I were taller. I want to find a ladder, prop it against the stone pedestal, and run my fingers over the apostle's weathered face. I want, irrationally, to make sure the monsoon doesn't wash the red paint off his finger. I know that Thomas is meant to look majestic here on this hilltop, elevated above his peers and even his Lord. But there is no church to shelter him here. No temple, no shrine, no candles and flowers to soften the wind and rain battering his body. Maybe this *is* Thomas as he really was two thousand years ago: alone, vulnerable, and far from home. A stranger in a strange land, driven into exile by a story so transformative and so compelling that he had no choice but to share it.

I have zero experience praying to saints. I don't know what to call him, or how to begin. I glance over my shoulder first, to make sure my family is out of earshot. But then I look into his eyes again, and the words come fast and without volition: "You believed and you doubted. You searched and you wandered. You know what it's like to be an outsider. You know what it is to yearn for home, for faith, for belonging. St. Thomas, Apostle of India, pray for me."

2 | NOWHERE TO LAY HIS HEAD: LEAVING

My mother was twenty-three years old when she landed in Schaffhausen, Switzerland, with a small suitcase, a few rupees, and a thick Indian accent. She was a newlywed, following my father from rural South India to the country that sponsored him to attend seminary. For a few years, as Dad studied Scripture and theology and church history, my mother studied the snow-capped mountains rimming the town, the blond, blue-eyed people who towered a good foot and a half over her, the endless varieties of cheese. She also studied the highs and lows of immigrant life: the yearning, curiosity, dislocation, and loss that haunt people who leave their homelands.

After my father graduated, my parents moved again, this time to the United States, and once again, they struggled to find their bearings in a new place. Much of the struggle was economic, social, and cultural. How would they survive financially? Who would their friends be? How would they bear the shock of racial prejudice? What would it take to raise Indian children in a culture they didn't understand, thousands of miles away from the wisdom of their elders?

Beneath all these struggles was a spiritual one. My parents had come of age in an intimate Christian subculture within South India. The Bible they loved, the hymns that formed them, the sermons they were accustomed to hearing: all were rooted in the cadences of their mother tongue, Malayalam, and the settings of small, close-knit villages in rural Kerala. How would they practice their faith in authentic ways in a country and language so different from their own? What would worship feel like in a new place, among new people? How, in the ancient words of the psalmist, would they learn to sing the Lord's songs in a foreign land? (Psalm 137:4).

The questions that hounded my parents in those early years in America—the questions I inherited even before I had the capacity to articulate them—were steeped in need and fear. The need to belong, feel safe, settle down. The fear of isolation, exposure, exile.

Some days, when I look back on my family's early years in the United States, I wish that we'd found an easier way forward. I wish I could say, "It didn't stay hard. We put down roots, forged new identities, and transitioned smoothly into American life and American Christianity."

But that's not the case. We struggled. I still struggle. As first-generation immigrants, my parents carried the loss of their ethnic and spiritual homeland in their bones, and they reacted as human beings often do in the face of difficult transitions. They approached their new reality with defensiveness and fear. They tried to recreate their nadhe in a culture that wouldn't accommodate it. They worked (in vain) to protect me from becoming what I was destined to become the moment they left India: an outsider. As a second-generation Asian American, I continue to find my experience of straddling two cultures challenging and lonely.

At the same time, I've come to see that this dual life is a gift. It shapes my faith in ways I wouldn't trade. Though it hurts at times, I've learned the high value of standing apart and in between, of holding paradox as a sacred gift, of accepting my "foreignness" as a pathway to spiritual growth.

The immigrant way, it turns out, is a sacred way.

———

In the Gospel of Matthew, a scribe approaches Jesus with great eagerness, promising to follow him anywhere. But Jesus pushes back on the scribe's naivete with a single, stunning line: "Foxes have holes, and birds of the air have nests; but the Son of Man has nowhere to lay his head" (8:19–20).

Every time I read this line of Scripture, the Jesus of two thousand years ago draws very near, and all I want is to listen to him. I want to hear *how* this aching line leaves his mouth. Does his voice tremble? Does his admission—even as he articulates it so bluntly—surprise even him? I wonder, because it surprises me. The Son of God, the Incarnate One, the second person of the Trinity: *homeless?*

There is much to say about Jesus's poverty from a material, economic, and social justice standpoint. The fact that God chooses to come to earth as a poor, colonized person with no access to worldly power speaks volumes about the kind of Sovereign we worship. We dare not minimize what this choice reveals about God's heart and priorities. When we care for the poor, the unhoused, the economically vulnerable, we are coming as close as we can to serving Jesus himself. He says as much: "Just as you did it to one of the least of these who are members of my family, you did it to me" (Matthew 25:40). Scripture does not romanticize Jesus's poverty, and neither should we.

But there is a spiritual wisdom to be found in his circumstances as well. What does it mean to follow a God who has no home, no place of belonging—a God who decides to experience our world as a traveler, a migrant, a wanderer, a guest? What does an intentional homelessness of heart and mind teach us about the radical power of vulnerability?

Part of what startles me about Jesus's response to the scribe is that it's not literally true. Jesus *does* have a home. He has a home in Nazareth. His childhood home, the home of his mother, father, and siblings. It's a home he returns to, according to Matthew, Mark, and Luke. So why does he describe himself as homeless?

According to the New Testament stories, Jesus's experience of homegoing is painful and rough. If we take it seriously, it might complicate our own relationships with the places we like to call home. In Matthew's version, Jesus's townspeople find him "altogether too much for them" (13:57, *The Inclusive Bible*). In Mark's version, Jesus's relatives attempt to stage an intervention, thinking that he has lost his mind. In Luke's version, Jesus infuriates his old friends and relations so thoroughly that they try to shove him over a cliff.

Somehow, just as Jesus comes into a deeper comprehension of his vocation and ministry, his home ceases to be the place where he can lay his head. Jesus can't go home again. The hometown boy can't make good.

I want to linger over Luke's version of the story, because its tension and drama reveal some of the complexities involved in leaving and returning home. Why, in the space of ten verses of Scripture, does everything go south? How does the affectionate curiosity of Jesus's Nazarene kin morph into rage and violence?

The story doesn't start out badly. When Jesus first stands up to read and speak in his childhood synagogue, his listeners are blown away by his gracious words and authoritative bearing. Is this really Joseph's boy? The neighborhood kid with the iffy birth story? Look how well he's turned out! Who would have thought he'd become a healer, a preacher, a miracle worker? Nazareth's very own rising star.

When I picture this scene, I imagine the townspeople waiting outside the local synagogue, itching to welcome Jesus home. They're curious. They want to know if the rumors about his greatness are true. They've heard the stories, of course: Stories of a descending dove and a voice like thunder. Stories of water turning to wine, of cures and exorcisms, feasts and resurrections. If the townspeople's native son is willing to peddle such miracles to strangers, how much more will he perform at home! Among his kin. His insiders. His favorites.

But those "favorites" turn out to be wrong. As Luke tells it, the story turns precisely when Jesus refuses to "go home" in the ways that matter most to his kin. He refuses to *be* at home. To *stay* at home. To allow his home to define him. Everything goes wrong when Jesus turns to his own and says, essentially: "I am not yours. I don't belong to you. I am not yours to claim, contain, or define."

Jesus does this by citing God's long history of prioritizing the outsider, the foreigner, and the stranger. Elijah was sent to care for the widow at Zarephath, he reminds them; he wasn't sent to the widows of Israel. Elisha was instructed to heal Naaman the Syrian, not the numerous people with leprosy in Israel. In other words, God has always been in the business of working on the margins. Of crossing borders. Of doing new things in remote and unlikely places. Far from home. Far from the familiar and the comfortable. Far from the centers of power and piety.

In Luke's account, it is *Jesus* who pushes his own people away and rejects his extended family's version of welcome. Refusing to accept their conditional hospitality, Jesus is the one who overturns their notions of home and of God's place in it.

"I *can't* come home in the way you expect me to," is the painful message he bears. "And you can't, either. You can't hunker down and stay where you are, expecting God to linger in the cozy and the familiar. God is on the move. God is doing a new thing. God is speaking in places you don't recognize as sacred, privileging voices you're not interested in hearing, and saying things that will make your ears burn. Can you handle it? God is not yours. *You are God's.*"

With the benefit of historical hindsight, we may find it easy to criticize the hotheaded people who accuse Jesus of heresy and expel him from their midst. I don't excuse their violence, but I see them as people trying to maintain stability in a dangerous and chaotic world. They crave order. They need their hierarchies. They want to uphold the traditions they cherish. What they *don't* want is to make waves. They're not out to thwart God; they just want to keep their world predictable and safe.

I can relate to this desire so well, which means I can't ponder this story of homegoing without wondering what it means for my own life. If the Jesus I worship fits too perfectly into my tribe, then is it really Jesus I'm worshipping? The Jesus in Luke's Gospel pushes so hard against his listeners' cherished assumptions about belonging that they nearly kill him. Does Jesus ever make *us* this angry? Does he prod at whatever it is we consider sacrosanct—our conservatism, our progressivism, our theology, our denomination, our biblical literacy, our prayer life, our politics, our wokeness—and ask us to leave it behind to follow him? If so, how do we respond?

I fear that church folks are the modern-day equivalent of Jesus's ancient townspeople. Those of us who belong to churches are often the ones who think we know Jesus the best, which makes us the ones most in danger of domesticating him. What will it take for us to follow him into new and uncomfortable territory? To see him where we least desire to look? To leave home?

In all three Gospel accounts of his return to Nazareth, Jesus chooses movement over stasis, change over security. He doesn't allow anyone to box him into an identity that's narrow and constricting. When the pious of his day attempt to "kill" the new and the unfamiliar, he chooses instead to lean into newness with curiosity and delight. Throughout his ministry, he allows himself and the people he encounters to *become*. To grow. To leave.

I wonder if we're like Jesus, or if we cut ourselves and others off with expectations none of us can bear: "You will *always* be small, weak, broken, insufficient, disappointing. You will *never* overcome your background, family, upbringing, wounds, addictions. Why can't you be obliging, accommodating, domesticated, *mine?*"

Sometimes, as Thomas Merton once wrote, we need to be "jerked clean out of the habitual." It is one of the most painful things that can happen to us. But it is also the very thing that might save us.

———————

The creatures of the earth, Jesus tells the eager scribe back in Matthew, have homes that tether them to their surroundings.

Homes that shelter them, homes that define their boundaries. But Jesus? Jesus has nothing of the sort. No bed, no table, no room, no roof, no shelter, no haven. No place in the world to call his own.

Every time I read these words, I feel a too-familiar sadness. The sadness of not-belonging. The grief of my grandparents, who stayed behind in India to preserve a nadhe that was destined to change no matter what. The sadness of my parents, who bore the psychological and cultural brunt of leaving. My own sadness at finding myself betwixt and between.

In the years since I left evangelicalism, this sadness has been a constant companion. My grief sits right alongside the fear that I'm a traitor: a culturally disloyal daughter to the long and storied religious heritage that formed me. No matter where I go, I wrestle with this sense of betrayal. Isn't it ungrateful to walk away? Isn't it selfish? Isn't it arrogant?

It's all too easy to allow this grief to dominate my faith. If I'm not attentive and careful, I can give myself over to a permanent sense of "too muchness." As in: I'm too Indian, too American, too feminine, too feminist, too pious, too skeptical, too earnest, too jaded to be in a Christian community at all.

I wonder if Jesus feels this way when his visit to Nazareth falls apart. Perhaps he worries that he's betraying his family by choosing a spiritual path they don't understand. The next time he interacts with his mother, maybe they talk about the shame he's caused her among their neighbors, and her embarrassment grieves him. Surely there are moments when he wishes that his path could be less costly, less treacherous.

Whenever the cost of my own leaving feels acute, it helps me to think of Jesus as bicultural, belonging at once in heaven and on earth. In Nazareth and outside of it. In choosing to draw near to us, he straddles a tremendous both-and, and he lives into that dissonance with love, patience, curiosity, and long-suffering.

———————

Jesus's plight is not unique in Scripture. Character after character, story after story, and text after text point to the spiritual value—even the spiritual *necessity*—of wandering, migrating, journeying, traveling. The Bible is full of people facing exile and braving return. People yearning to belong while standing apart. People hitting the road with nothing to hang onto but God.

Adam and Eve leave their garden home to learn the complexities of relationship with their Creator. Noah and his family become boat people. Abram and Sarai say goodbye to their ancestral home in order to experience God's abundant promise.

It's when Hagar is cast into the desert that she names God, becoming the first human being in the Bible to do so. Jacob sees visions of the Divine while on the run from his brother. Joseph is cast out of his homeland before he can save it. Moses discerns his vocation in exile, far from the comforts of Pharaoh's court.

The Israelites wander in the wilderness for forty years before God deems them ready for a new home. Elijah hears God's evocative silence when he flees to a cave. Ruth becomes Jesus's ancestor because she's willing to become an immigrant. Jonah learns the hard lessons of mercy in an alien land he loathes. The Israelites relearn their hunger for God during the Babylonian exile.

Mary, then, gives birth in a stable, far away from her own mother and closest kin. She and Joseph cross national borders to shield their child from state-sponsored slaughter.

The disciples of Jesus leave their nets, their boats, their family members, and their livelihoods to find their vocations. The first seventy-two Christian missionaries learn their trade on the road, in the seminary of not-belonging.

In Jesus's parables, the lost son is the one who finds himself. The lost lamb is the one the shepherd saves. The great commission Jesus issues is not "Therefore, hunker down." It is "Therefore, *go*" (Matthew 28:19).

After the resurrection and ascension, an Ethiopian eunuch finds their salvation far from home. Paul encounters Jesus on the road to Damascus, a blazing liminal space of judgment and grace. Jesus's fledgling followers scatter when Stephen is martyred, seeding the first great flowering of the church. John of Patmos pens the book of Revelation in exile.

In short, much of the Bible is written by, for, and about wanderers. Clearly, there is something powerful, instructive, and transformative about leaving home. About being an outsider. About exploring the contours of faith from the margins. What does it mean that our holy book is filled with wanderers and misfits, pilgrims and desert dwellers, refugees and immigrants?

At some deep, wise level, the writers of Scripture recognize that there is merit in the perspective of the outsider: one who can move in and through, between and out, noticing, connecting, reordering, and straddling the gap. Jesus himself straddles the vast gap between humanity and divinity. At a more granular level, he straddles the gap between firstborn son and itinerant preacher. Between those who love him and those who hate him. Between the demands of his friends and followers and his need for solitude and rest. Even when it costs him dearly, he chooses to occupy an in-between place, and in doing so, he renders it more spacious for us. The immigrant way is a sacred way.

My mother is in her late seventies now, but I still imagine her all those years ago, stepping off a plane into a new world—a young, vibrant woman full of hope and fear. She had no idea what her family would navigate in the decades that followed. She wanted to *arrive*. We all did. How were we to know that arrival isn't the point?

3 | INTO THE WILDERNESS: LOST

I am not sure how I functioned before the invention of GPS. My husband and I are twenty-seven years into our marriage, and he *still* jokes about how we spent a good portion of our honeymoon lost in the Blue Ridge Mountains because I couldn't make heads or tails out of a road atlas or a trail map. It's almost formulaic, how I'll turn left when I'm supposed to turn right or insist that I'm heading north as I speed down a southbound highway.

Now that I live in the age of Waze and Google Maps, I fare better. Until I don't. Sometimes a storm hits, or a tree falls, or a fellow driver on a winding country road suffers an accident and the way ahead of me closes. Sometimes when this happens, my handy digital navigator fails to register the interruption in real time, and I find myself taking long, unfamiliar detours with no reliable guidance.

Suddenly, the majestic redwoods lining the road turn ominous. My grip on the steering wheel tightens. My heart beats a little too fast. I look helplessly at my iPhone, willing one of its apps to solve my predicament. I don't like being lost.

For many of us, a similar anxiety hounds our spiritual lives. We fear leaving the religious homes we know best—even when those homes become cramped and oppressive—because we dread getting lost. We're not used to hitting the road without a familiar guide to chart out each turn. Some of us even associate lostness with sinfulness: "I *once* was lost, but *now* am found, was blind, but now I see," John Newton wrote in his famous hymn. Being lost and getting lost are things we do *before* we put our faith in Jesus, we think. Not after.

The irony is that in Scripture, God is closest to those who are lost. To know the God of the Bible is to know a perpetual searcher, seeker, pursuer, and finder. God doesn't stay put with the comfortably "housed"; God is the shepherd who leaves the ninety-nine in search of the one. God is the housewife with a broom, peering through the cobwebs, exploring the corners, and rattling the rafters for her lost coin. God is the prodigal father, extravagant and ridiculous in his love for the boy who runs away. We don't have to worry that getting lost will separate us from God, because God lives where the lost things are.

In fact, getting lost might be the best way for us to learn how to live and love as God desires. In her book *An Altar in the World*, Barbara Brown Taylor describes a command that runs through the five books of the Torah. "There are many variations on it, given in very many contexts, but the basic gist of it is, 'You shall love the stranger, for you were strangers in the land of Egypt,'" she writes. "Those most likely to befriend strangers, in other words, are those who have been strangers themselves. The best way to grow empathy for those who are lost is to know what it means to be lost yourself."

I know from my own experiences of spiritual wandering that Taylor is right. Lostness softens the heart. It makes us more attentive and generous toward the lostness of others. It's only when we've left the protective shelters of our belonging and experienced how it feels to be the stranger, the foreigner, the misfit, the newcomer, that we can truly empathize with those on the margins.

Lostness is what happens when we walk away from our first inheritance, our first culture, our first home with God. When I left evangelicalism, I felt like I was entering a wilderness in the darkest hours of the night. The right way had disappeared, and I'd stumbled into a dense forest, full of unknown dangers. The terror was ominous and total; all I felt was dread. I strained against the shadows of maybe-trees, maybe-monsters, appalled that nothing looked familiar. I waited for anything recognizable, anything friendly, to orient me. Nothing appeared.

It took a long time to remember that the forest is actually more than dangerous. To ask: What else do I know about the woods at night? What gifts might this lostness offer?

Eventually, I noticed the softness of the pine needles under my feet. The benign company of an owl, a squirrel, a deer. The dying embers of my own campfire. The layers upon layers of stars, collapsing space and time with singular pinpricks of light.

At that point, I had a decision to make. Would I dismiss these gifts out of hand and still try to flee the wilderness? Or would I pause long enough to give thanks?

If we dare to leave home and stick it out on the journey of faith, we must lean into the possibility of lostness, and trust the God of lost things to find us. We have to slow down long enough to take in the austere beauty of the dark road in the woods.

Maybe we'll decide that the darkness of the night is holy. We'll name it. Welcome it. Hold open our hands and offer it our consent: "I have come. I am here. I will take another step forward. Then another. Then another."

The real journey begins when we learn to pay attention—not a vigilant, frightened attention but a curious one. Our eyes adjust, and we make our peace with the one thing we know: We are here now. In this wood, amid these trees. Not forever. But now. And that is enough. Because God is here, too.

———

It's instructive that we feel so much pressure in American Christianity to house ourselves. Like the eleven-year-olds in the School of Witchcraft and Wizardry of the Harry Potter series, we want so badly to be done with Sorting. We want to don the hat and find out exactly where we belong theologically, doctrinally, scripturally. As if those are things fixed in stone. As if they can't shift or evolve.

The Gospel of Luke records a challenging story about the spiritual homes we often cling to. Jesus and his friends are walking in the temple complex in Jerusalem one day when someone stops to admire the temple's architectural glory. "Look at the beautiful stones and pillars," they say. "What solid craftsmanship! What beautiful handiwork!"

To call the temple in first-century Jerusalem an "achievement" would be an understatement. It was a *massive* complex: roughly three football fields wide and five football fields long. Each one of its enormous foundation stones measured forty feet. It had sprawling courtyards, sweeping porches, covered walkways, and a monumental staircase. King Herod reportedly used so much silver and gold to cover the façade of the temple's main entrance that it would blind anyone who gazed at it in bright sunlight.

More importantly, the temple represented the most unshakable symbol of God's presence that the Jewish people of Jesus's day could imagine. As a colonized people, bristling under the cruelties of the Roman Empire, they clung to the temple as a refuge. A fist in the air. A promise of vindication and victory. For them, the temple offered unwavering proof that the God of their ancestors was still their God.

But Jesus's response to his gushing friend is a shocking downer: "As for these things that you see, the days will come when not one stone will be left upon another; all will be thrown down" (Luke 21:6).

I imagine there was stunned silence after Jesus said this.

We all have places we consider sacred—places that hold spiritual meaning and memory, that tug at our hearts and enliven us with fresh experiences of God. These are the churches, cathedrals, retreat centers, family cabins, beaches, or secluded spots in the forest where we've found refuge, or wrestled our way to a new comprehension of our belovedness, or grieved something precious, or been saved by beauty.

How would we feel if Jesus met us in that holy place and said, "See this? See *all of this?* It's not going to last; it's going to come crashing down. Every beam, every pillar, every nook, every window, every painting, every icon, every tree, every riverbed. Not one stone will be left upon another."

What would we say? What would we do?

Jesus tells his listeners that the temple in Jerusalem, which is the heart and center of their worship and their identity, will fall to ruins before their eyes. Where they see beauty, he sees rubble. Where they see permanence, he sees change. Where they see security, he sees the necessity of death before resurrection.

In Luke's apocalyptic text, Jesus looks up at that stunning edifice and calls it a ruin. Which is to say, he invites his friends to consider the possibility that God is up to something much bigger than their beloved temple. That the divine work of salvation, justice, healing, and mercy won't be domesticated—not in mortar and stone, not in icon and stained glass, not even in our cherished conceptions of what counts as holy ground. That God in God's vast generosity and creativity will exceed every edifice, every institution, every mission statement, and every high place we create in God's name—and that God will invite us to exceed them, too.

If this remains true for us today—and I believe it does—we need to ask ourselves some hard questions: What spiritual homes or identities do we clench in both fists, believing that our faith will not survive outside of them? How might we domesticate God instead of letting Love loose to do its astonishing work in the wide world? Can we remain standing even when our beautiful homes fall apart and we are forced out into the wilderness?

Less than forty years after Jesus stood in the temple and predicted its destruction, the Roman legions attacked Jerusalem and tore that magnificent house of worship to the ground. Not one stone was left upon another.

When I imagine that catastrophic scene, I picture the writers of the Gospels—Luke and his faith community among them—standing in those smoking ruins and somehow finding the courage to bear witness. Asking each other, perhaps, what it all meant. What it was all for.

"Was it worth it?" they might have asked each other. "Leaving? Following Jesus? Venturing into unknown, uncharted territory? Was it worth it?"

Christians believe in a community of saints, centuries old, who decided that the answer was yes. Yes, it was worth it. Even when the walls fell, it was worth it. Even when the unmarked road stretched out before us, it was worth it.

I wonder what we'll say when our turn comes.

Luke's story ends with a promise: "By your endurance you will gain your souls" (21:19). Which is to say, the church is not a building or an institution. It can't be contained within walls— even beautiful, exquisitely crafted walls. The church is the love of God working through the endurance, tenacity, and openness of God's people. The church is the witness we agree to bear even when empires rise and fall.

———————

That said, there *is* a kind of lostness, a kind of self-inflicted exile, that doesn't serve the spiritual life well. It's a version that refuses to engage along the way. That refuses to love the journey or the lands through which we move. It's a version that looks perpetually backward, lost in longing, nostalgia, and self-pity.

Growing up in a community of South Asian immigrant families, I saw firsthand the damage a fear-based exile can cause. I saw parents who were so afraid of American culture that they refused to let their children participate in it at all. I saw children, in turn, break under the pressure to hold themselves apart from the American schools, neighborhoods, and friends they wanted to love. I saw families spend years hovering over the United States, their new country, for fear of contamination, never quite landing, never quite making it their own. This new world they found themselves in was too strange and too scary—too unlike what they'd known and loved. So they refused to inhabit it. They spoke ill of it. They *willed* their hearts to keep in a holding pattern and never land.

But this kind of intentional not-belonging hardens, atrophies, and curls us inward. It makes us unloving toward the places in which we find ourselves. Everything becomes a threat. A rejection. An assault. We absolutize our own preferred homes, cultures, traditions, and spiritualities, and we forget that God's kingdom is larger than the tiny nooks and crannies of the world we inhabit.

I think of Jeremiah 29:7 as a useful and necessary corrective: "Seek the welfare of the city where I have sent you into exile . . . for in its welfare you will find your welfare." When it comes to our spiritual lives, God rejects the binary of retreating or assimilating—and so should we. We should love the stops along the way. Love the pathways, the byways, the way stations of our lostness and not-belonging. When Jesus has "no place to lay his head," he commits himself to the welfare of each village he visits, each home he steps into, each synagogue he enters, each person with whom he strikes up a conversation. He is not a tourist, as he doesn't approach his surroundings as a careless consumer. He doesn't see his life on earth as a vacation, as time off from something else that's more "real."

Instead, he approaches life as a pilgrim. He recognizes that every place is sacred, that it has the capacity to teach and form us, even for a short period of time. He knows that the foreign lands he wanders through are not foreign to God. They are places God loves, places God desires to heal and transform into the beloved community, God's kingdom, God's dream.

"To live in the world as a pilgrim," writes seminary professor Chris Armstrong, "is to hold things, and places, and even people, lightly—enjoying them all in God, not as gods. For the nature of sin is not that we love bad things, but that we love good things as if they were final things."

I believe we're called to a posture of *full presence*. We're called to love the "cities" we travel through, to seek their welfare, to love them with every ounce of our beings even as we hold them lightly, knowing that the road is long and winding. We're called to value the road itself, the traveling, the wandering, the navigating. This kind of faith takes change as a given, not as something to avoid and fear. It encourages us to pare down, to shed excess, to lighten our loads. What is really essential? What is extraneous? What will make the next stretch of this journey meaningful?

A sedentary spirituality, on the other hand, refuses to let go, refuses to travel. It renders us inflexible around religious customs and traditions. It strips us of all theological or spiritual curiosity. It deceives us into believing we've arrived—that we have nothing else to learn, and nowhere else to go. We hunker down, trying to protect the territory we deem to be ours. We live in fear. Fear of the religious or spiritual other. Fear of change. Fear of contamination. Fear of a slippery slope. As in: If I surrender *this* cherished tradition, belief, assumption, or practice, I might lose everything! If I dare to read the Bible differently than I have before, it might cease to resonate as God's Word. If I experiment with a new style of worship, I might lose the warmth and intimacy of God's presence. If I pray using a new name or visual image for the Divine, I might offend God. If I cross denominational lines, I might slip into heresy. We think of our faith as beads on a string. If one bead slips, they'll all slip, fall, and scatter across the floor. So we freeze in place instead.

Whether this inertia comes over us in a conservative evangelical guise ("I accepted Jesus into my heart as my personal Savior years ago") or a progressive, mainline one ("I was baptized as a baby and confirmed as a teenager"), it shrinks the expansive spiritual life God has for us. It leaves us in the shallows, when what God desires for us is intimacy in the depths.

So, is the destination important, or is it the path that matters? *Yes.* The answer is yes. The destination shapes the path. The path makes possible the destination. We can't have one without the other. It's when we dare to hit the road that we learn how to be good guests, how to receive care and nurture in a culture that often looks down on need as weakness. It's the traveler wandering in strange territory who recognizes her need for friendship and connection. It's the pilgrim who must learn to approach with gentleness, with a willingness to listen and learn—not to dominate the conversation or to insist that he knows everything there is to know. An immigrant's work is to be open, curious, and flexible. To trust that there are no "God-forsaken" countries, places, or homes, because God is everywhere, and God will meet us anywhere.

———

I can't write about lostness in the Christian tradition without naming the deepest fear: Some of us learned early on to associate lostness with *godlessness*, as if the worst thing that can happen is that we might wander into realms of actual unbelief. Of agnosticism or even atheism. I grew up reading, hearing, and pronouncing Scripture verses like Psalm 14:1: "Fools say in their hearts, 'There is no God.'" *I'd* never wander *that* far, I thought.

But of course I have. More than once. If my history is a fair predictor, I might again. For years, though, I wasn't honest enough to admit it. To admit that I've lost my faith at times. That I've said, "There is no God."

I've said it out of anguish, lost in the grief of unanswered prayer. I've said it in the face of global tragedies—tsunamis, earthquakes, famines, mass shootings—which mock the very idea of a benevolent deity. I've said it in loneliness, living as I do in a post-Christian culture that takes for granted God's nonexistence. I've said it in bewilderment, because God is invisible and I often experience God mostly as a sweet but aching absence. There are days when my pursuit of the Presence-That-Is-Absence makes me tired. Makes me angry. Makes me doubtful. Makes me quit.

But if a Christian has never—not even once—sat with the possibility that there is no God, then I believe she hasn't sat long enough with the world's brokenness and horror. He hasn't allowed the real stories of real people to sear his soul. They haven't knelt long enough at the cross.

Among my friends and acquaintances who aren't believers, I don't hear much in the way of arrogance when they dismiss the possibility of God's existence. I hear frustration over religious institutions rife with hypocrisy. I hear impatience with canned language and false cheer—the Christianese that flattens life into caricature. And I hear pain—the pain of yearning for faith and finding it unavailable.

I have to admit that my own faith is a mystery. I don't know why I keep circling back to belief. I don't know why my forays into agnosticism and atheism have been infrequent and brief. Skeptics might say my upbringing in a Christian family has primed me for belief: that is, that faith is the default setting, built into my mental architecture. Or they might say my faith is a product of my weakness: that I'm frail and broken, and that faith provides the crutch I need to make survival possible.

Maybe. Or maybe faith is an unfathomable gift, given at the discretion of a Giver whose ways I can't predict or quantify.

———

When I was little, the family vacations that didn't take us to India involved long road trips around the United States. Every summer, my father would invite extended family members—aunts, uncles, cousins—to join us, and we'd pack everyone into a fifteen-passenger van and hit the road for a week. Toronto; Niagara Falls; Washington, DC; and Disney World are some of the places we visited.

What I remember more clearly than the destinations, though, is the food we ate along the way. Before each trip, my mom would hole up in her kitchen with a few of my aunts, preparing a spectacular assortment of snacks and meals for the road. Fried plantains and banana chips; rice flour–based breads like appams and idlis; dosas stuffed with spicy potatoes; crispy lentil patties called vadas; chicken biryani wrapped in single-serving aluminum foil pockets; and sweet cardamom cake for dessert.

These were our journeying foods, and they made up at least half the fun (and the mess!) of each summer adventure. Sometimes we'd eat in the van, passing brown paper bags of banana chips and vadas back and forth between the rows of seats. Sometimes my father would pull over to a rest stop, my mother would spread a bedsheet out on the grass, and we'd feast right there by the highway.

On none of those trips did it occur to my parents to get takeout at McDonald's. Preparing, serving, and sharing our own journeying foods—foods rich in cultural associations, family memories, and cherished scents and flavors—was an essential part of our vacations.

Those journeys were leisurely ones, and the foods that accompanied them were consumed lightheartedly and with pleasure. But I remember other journeys, too, sustained by other journeying foods. The night we learned that my grandfather had died suddenly, necessitating my mother's emergency flight back to India to attend his funeral, my aunts streamed into our house. As Mom mourned and cried and packed, they stuffed warm Tupperware dishes of food into her carry-on luggage. They wanted her to eat something. *Anything.* They wanted her to feel nourished even as she grieved.

I remember the treacherous drives my father would sometimes make for work during icy Boston winters, the flasks of strong coffee my mother always brewed for him, to keep him alert behind the wheel. I remember the huge pots of stew my parents brought to my house when I was recovering from childbirth— sore, hormonal, tired, and overwhelmed by my colicky newborn. "To build your strength back up," my mother said each time she handed me a steaming bowl and insisted that I empty it. "Motherhood is a long journey. You need to be strong."

In a story told in the book of 1 Kings, the prophet Elijah finds himself on a journey of his own—an arduous journey filled with peril and terror. He has just defeated the prophets of Baal in a dramatic showdown on a mountaintop, and now he's on the run from the furious Queen Jezebel, who wants him dead. After hours of running, he finally collapses under a broom tree. He prays for a while, literally asking God to kill him so that he won't have to face the hardships of one more day. And then he falls asleep.

What follows is one of the most gentle and tender passages in the Hebrew Bible. Elijah awakens to the touch of an angel, who tells him to get up and eat. When Elijah looks around, he sees that the angel has prepared a cake baked on hot stones, and a jar of water, for him to eat and drink. Elijah, still sleepy and despondent, nibbles and sips. But not to the angel's satisfaction. She rouses him again: "Get up and eat, otherwise the journey will be too much for you" (19:7). At her second invitation, Elijah obeys in earnest, and his strength is renewed. The story goes on to note that the prophet perseveres on his journey after he eats the angel's cake. In fact, he's able to endure for forty days and forty nights on the nourishment of that one meal.

There's so much to love about this story. I love that the angel meets Elijah in the wilderness, just as he's losing hope and refusing to take another step forward. I love that she offers not advice, not a sermon, not platitudes, but *cake*. I love that she insists on him eating his fill.

And I absolutely love that the angel never minimizes or dismisses the difficulties of Elijah's journey. Of faith *as journey*. As exile. As desert wandering. She never says, "Get over yourself, Elijah; your situation isn't so bad." Or "You've survived the worst of it, I promise; it'll all be downhill from now on." Or "Once you eat what I've prepared for you, things will be smooth and easy. You'll be blessed and safe and rich and happy. You'll never experience fear or sadness again."

No. She says, "The journey is hard. It's *hard.* You won't ever make it on your own. But you don't have to. Here's cake. Here's sustenance. Here's journeying bread. Get up and eat it. You can't sidestep the journey you're called to; it belongs to you. But you *can* choose how you make it: Famished or fed. Strengthened or weak. Accompanied or alone. Which will you choose?"

Whenever I peer down the road of my Christian life and feel overwhelmed at the prospect of setting forth or getting lost one more time, I remember these stories of journeying bread. My mother with her neat, fragrant brown-paper parcels. An angel baking bread over hot stones and prodding its warmth into an exhausted prophet's mouth. Bread for hope. Bread for the long haul. Bread for all who dare to walk the way of the cross.

In the Gospels, Jesus compares himself to manna, another ancient and powerful journeying bread. Manna sustains the Israelites in their long wilderness, just as the angel's cake sustains Elijah in his. I believe Jesus desires to sustain us in ours, to be our journeying bread for every road trip, every leave-taking, every perilous ride, every long haul. He desires to be our comfort, our joy, our nourishment, our delight, our substance, and our strength—and not in some magical, cure-all way, but in ways that meet us in our real lives, our real challenges, our real fears and griefs and hopes.

Because the one who had no place to lay his head knows better than anyone that the journey is hard. The one who spent forty days in the lostness of the wilderness knows we can't handle the shadowy landscape on our own. He knows we need bread that sustains. His bread. His flesh. Given for the life of the world. *Get up and eat.*

4 | BEYOND BELIEF: STORY

If you could live in a story, which one would you choose? My husband and I started asking our children this question when they were preschoolers. Every night, our son and daughter would curl up on our bed in their pajamas, their hair still damp from their baths, and we'd spread their favorite library books around us. They would beg for one more story, or two more, or three. We'd read aloud, often long past their bedtime, imagining ourselves in all kinds of fictional worlds.

In the early years, we'd debate the merits of Winnie the Pooh's Hundred Acre Wood over Robin Hood's Sherwood Forest, or compare Peter Pan's Neverland to Dr. Seuss's Whoville, or pretend we lived in a pigpen under Charlotte's famous web.

As the kids' reading abilities grew, so did our imagined destinations. Over the years, we cycled through Narnia, Wonderland, Terabithia, and Oz. For a while, my daughter's heroine was Anne of Green Gables, so we "lived" on Prince Edward Island and bemoaned our carrot-colored hair. My son's hero for a long while was Harry Potter, so we spent equal time at Hogwarts Castle, learning spells and playing Quidditch. Our Middle Earth phase lasted for years, and required many, many decisions about Tolkien's elaborate story-world: Would we live in Rivendell or the Shire? Be elves, dwarves, hobbits, or humans? Venture into Mirkwood, visit Lothlorien, or hazard the long darkness of Moria?

One day when my son was around twelve, he looked up from whatever book he was reading and said, "I hope heaven has a good story. Does God write good ones? 'Forever' will be boring otherwise."

I can't remember now what half-baked answer I gave him, but I do remember that the question stopped me in my tracks. Does God write good stories? What did it mean to ask that? I felt as if two strictly separate parts of my life had crashed into each other at ninety miles per hour. Christianity might be a *story?*

Over the next weeks and months, my son's comment churned inside me. Something awakened: A possibility. A yearning. A hope. I thought about how intuitively human beings turn to stories to make sense of our lives, and I wondered why no one had ever explained my faith to me in such immersive, inviting terms. What did it mean that in every other area of my life, I warmed to narrative, plot, arc, and drama? Even as I hungered for context, reveled in metaphor, and crafted endless chains of cause and effect to make sense of most of my world, why was my religious life an exception?

Storytelling is one of the oldest and most universal forms of human communication. Stories are gifts we pass on from one generation to the next. Stories hold memory and identity, seasons and secrets, sorrows and joys. They give our lives texture and depth, roundness and fullness.

Even the opening words of the book that Christians hold sacred are classic story words: "In the beginning." The Bible is full of rich, colorful, and multilayered narratives no less compelling than the novels and short-story collections that have pride of place on my bookshelves. Jesus himself taught almost exclusively in parables, which are merely short stories.

Far more than we human beings love propositions and principles, we love leaning in to hear a good tale. What happened next? we ask. Why did she do that? Did the villain get his comeuppance? Will the heroine live happily ever after? How did it all end?

I knew all this long before my son asked me about God's stories, and yet I didn't see how this knowledge had anything to do with my spiritual life. I didn't consider the possibility that Christianity itself might be a story as exhilarating and nourishing as all the bedtime books I spent years exploring with my children.

Why is it so easy for so many of us to miss this truth? How do so many of us miss God's exquisite Story?

———————

I was twelve years old when my father baptized me. I remember the day very clearly: the summer sun reflecting on the water of a large outdoor swimming pool; church members, friends, and extended family leaning in close and singing "Nothing but the Blood of Jesus"; my father's hands covering mine as he lowered me into the cool water.

I also remember the words he used to pronounce what was happening in that pivotal moment of immersion: "Upon your profession of faith in the Lord Jesus Christ, and in obedience to his divine command, I baptize you in the name of the Father, and of the Son, and of the Holy Spirit."

In the Christian community that raised me, baptism testified to an individual's personal *belief.* Belief was the core of

Christianity, its living, beating heart. To enter into orthodox faith was to agree that certain theological statements about God, Jesus, the Holy Spirit, the human condition, the Bible, and the church were true. When the Christians around me spoke of "growing in the faith," what they meant was that they were honing and pruning their doctrinal commitments. To be a mature Christian was to have all of one's theological ducks in a row.

This honing, moreover, was a serious business. As a child, I watched congregations split up over the legitimacy of infant baptism over "believer's" baptism. I grew up around Christians who considered speaking in tongues, or refusing to wear jewelry, or staying away from beer and movie theaters, a litmus test for faith. I heard pastors fight over whether the communion table should be open (available to all) or closed (reserved for baptized members of a particular church). I heard others argue vociferously over details concerning the "great tribulation": Would God take Christians to heaven before the suffering of the end times, or would they have to hang around and endure the birth pains of a new kingdom too?

Accordingly, the questions I had to answer on that summer day before my father plunged me into the water were creedal questions—queries of intellectual assent to a set of very specific propositions. "Do you believe that there is only one God? Do you believe that Jesus is God's only begotten Son? Do you believe that Jesus died to save you from your sins? Do you believe that he rose again on the third day? Do you believe he will return someday to judge the living and the dead?"

It was essential that I understood the importance of these questions, and equally essential that I responded to them with a confident, unwavering "Yes!" After all, baptism was *my* promise to God. My signature on the dotted line of a contract called Belief.

A few years after my baptism, my high school physics teacher gave me a Petra CD, and I briefly became a Christian rock fan. My favorite Petra song was "Creed," an adaptation of the Apostles' Creed, set to an explosion of drums and guitars. The song moves between various "I believe" *statements* ("I believe in God the Father / maker of heaven and earth. / And in Jesus Christ, His only Son. / I believe in the virgin birth") and an emphatic chorus that ends with the line "And I will hold steadfast to this creed."

For months, I listened to "Creed" at top volume in my bedroom. If no one was home, I belted out the chorus with Petra's lead vocalist, Peter Shlitt, and prayed to feel the same assurance the band felt as they performed. I was hungry for certainty, for belonging, for *home*, and once again, as on the day of my baptism, the creed seemed to offer exactly what I needed.

Belief, in this strictly creedal sense, offered my anxious teenage self a set of clear borders and boundaries. "You may go this far, but no further." Belief-centered faith gave me rules, and the illusion of control, security, and immunity that comes with them. If I believed, I wouldn't have to wrestle with doubt, because every question that mattered would have an answer. And every question that didn't have an answer wouldn't matter.

If I believed, I wouldn't have to go looking for truth; truth became a bulleted list of propositions I could affirm and memorize. If I believed, I wouldn't have to "work out my salvation" as St. Paul suggests in his letter to the Philippians (2:12); I could just check off all the important boxes—"Virgin birth: check!" "Holy Trinity: check!" "Substitutionary atonement: check!"—and earn an A+ in the course called Faith. I wouldn't have to imagine my way into a coherent identity; religious creed would *be* my identity. "I, Debie, am a Bible-believing Christian. A follower of Jesus. A child of God. That is the sum total of who I am."

But of course, belief was *not* the sum total of who I was. I was so much more. We are *all* so much more. I was the kid who harbored questions no historic creed could answer: Is God white or brown? Indian or American? What language does God think in? Why does God have a Son and not a Daughter? What kind of heavenly Father kills his own Son to save wicked people? If women are made in God's image, why do they have to obey men? How will I be happy in heaven if other people are burning in hell? Why do I feel sorry for all the wrong people in the Bible? Job's wife. Queen Vashti. Lazarus. (What if he didn't *want* to be raised?) What about the Egyptian soldiers who drowned in the Red Sea?

My faith life was too weird-shaped to fit inside the linear logic of belief alone. Whether I could recite the Nicene Creed on Sunday mornings without crossing my fingers behind my back was neither here nor there. My inner life was too jagged and too raw for the church's "Have more faith!" platitudes.

As a teen, I had no idea that creeds are *meant* to restrict and exclude. A faith based on belief alone inevitably centers on rightness and wrongness, insiders and outsiders. Historically, creeds have always served this purpose; they were written to weed out heresy.

As I grew older, I began to see the "creed wars" as ugly, noxious, and harmful, both for the Christians engaged in them and for all of us watching from the sidelines. None of the religious debates I grew up hearing were funny or peripheral to the people who engaged in them. It was with perfect earnestness that they argued over the potential evils of ordaining women, or baptizing infants, or using inclusive language for God, or opening the communion table to spiritual seekers.

For me, such arguments felt worse than superfluous; they sucked the air right out of the room. In time, they diminished the faith I loved, making it narrower and narrower. Was the good news really so fragile and contingent? Would the religion actually crumble if women took the pulpit, or fell in love with each other? Did everything that matters in this vast universe come down to the book of Genesis versus a guy named Darwin? Was Christianity really so mingy? So small?

The problem with belief-centered Christianity is not that it's wrong. In fact, even though I don't enjoy Christian rock anymore, I still cherish the creeds. I love the moment in worship each Sunday morning when we stand to recite words that are ancient, rich, and sturdy. I love the power and beauty of public recitation. I love the creeds for their theological depth and their gorgeous poetry: "God from God, Light from Light, true God from true God." I love knowing that my affirmation unites me with a community of Christians spanning both time and space.

No, the problem is not that belief is *wrong*; it's that belief divorced from our enfleshed and storied lives is *not enough*. Because assenting to a set of propositions cannot foster the deep, all-encompassing relationship we desire to have with God. It cannot immerse us in a reality rich and textured enough for all our ideas, thoughts, questions, and hopes. If anything, intellectual assent is a smokescreen. A distraction. A thin, dissatisfying substitute for something much larger and more wonderful.

In her book *Christianity After Religion*, historian Diana Butler Bass writes that the English word *believe* comes from the German *belieben*—the German word for "love." To believe is not to hold an opinion. To believe is to love. To treasure. To cherish. To adore.

To believe in something is to invest it with love.

This is true in the ancient languages of the Bible as well. When the writers of the Hebrew Bible and the New Testament wrote of faithfulness, they were not writing about an intellectual surrender to a set of factual truths. They were writing about a trust, born of love, that is incarnate and full. Mind and body. Church and world. Theory and practice. They were writing about throwing themselves with abandon into the vastness of God. Faith as engagement, orientation, action. Faith as something we *do*.

Whenever I read the Gospels, I'm struck by how often and how lavishly Jesus commends the faith of those who seek him out. "Your faith has saved you," he tells a woman who anoints his feet, a Samaritan man with leprosy who returns to thank him, and a hemorrhaging woman who grasps his cloak (Luke 7:50; 17:19; Mark 5:34). "Your faith has made you well," he tells a blind beggar (Mark 10:52). "Such faith I have not seen in all of Israel!" he exclaims about a Roman centurion (Matthew 8:10).

What is it that Jesus admires in these people? As far as I can tell, the only thing they do is turn to him. Orient themselves in his direction. Trust him. What earns his admiration is their willingness, even in difficult, painful, and potentially risky circumstances, to dare a move toward love. To lean into Jesus's goodness, healing, justice, and mercy.

"If you had faith the size of a mustard seed," Jesus says to his disciples in Luke 17:6. As if to say, "You *do*. Don't you understand? You have faith already. This is not about proportion. I can't give you a recipe. We're not balancing chemical equations with a neutron here and two protons there. You have faith because you have me. You've seen me and known me. What else do you lack?"

Faith isn't fireworks; it's not meant to dazzle. Faith means recognizing our tiny place in relation to God's enormous, creative love and then filling that place with our whole lives.

On the day I got baptized, I had no sense that I was giving myself over to something bigger than myself. I had no idea that my personal decision to love God, important though it is, pales in significance to God's cosmic decision to love me—and the whole of humanity and creation along with me. Becoming a Christian, I thought, was all about *me* choosing Christ. Consequently, what I knew and felt as a young Christian was an almost overwhelming sense of responsibility. So much depended on my ability to keep believing! There was so much I needed to get right. So many ways I could mess up. Even years after my baptism, I feared for my salvation. Maybe my profession of faith hadn't been fervent enough when I got baptized, or maybe I had inadvertently crossed a line into heresy, or maybe my doctrine wasn't as pure as it should be.

But what if faith is less about me choosing Christ and more about Christ choosing me? What if the foundation of the Christian life is *Jesus's* faithfulness, not ours? It took me a long time to see that there is something wider, deeper, and more trustworthy I can stand on than the shifting sands of my own beliefs or even the particular practices and preferences of my denomination, ethnic tradition, or church. It didn't occur to me to trust the spaciousness of the sacred Story we live in—the Story of a Savior whose complete faithfulness to God's will has already thrown the doors of God's house wide open for all of us.

Even though I might believe and disbelieve a hundred times a day, the efficacy of my baptism—and my place in God's heart—holds. I am *held*. Not by my own profession of faith but by the saving power of the One who parts the clouds, blesses the water, and calls me a beloved child. It's not that I tether myself to a creed. It's that I enter into an entire story universe. An ancient cloud of witnesses. A worldwide community of the faithful. A liturgy that endures and evolves. A created universe that is wild and free as it whispers, laughs, and shouts God's name from every nook and cranny.

———————

Okay. So what? What if the beating heart of Christianity *is* story and not creed? What then? What happens to faith? To belief? If faith is a willingness to live within God's Story, what would it look like to do so?

We can begin by acquainting ourselves with a God who is much more welcoming, dynamic, and spirited than the God of abstract dogma. A storied God is a curious God, a listening God, an artistic God, a risk-taking God.

As New Testament scholar and theologian Daniel Kirk puts it, "God isn't above the fray." We don't serve a remote, disconnected God who chooses every once in a while to dip into the pages of our lives to add a line or a paragraph. Rather, what Scripture reveals is a God, Kirk writes, "who has so bound God's identity with [God's] people that what happens to them on earth is a reflection of God in heaven." God is more *in* this with us than God is standing apart and intervening from afar.

What Kirk calls a "storied theology" requires us to make connections we might not make otherwise. Christianity *as story* invites us to lead integrated lives, bringing together our Sunday pieties with our Monday questions, our Friday heartbreaks with our Saturday sins. Story reminds us that our present is always a patchwork; we are not static creatures. Like characters in a novel, we come from somewhere, and we're always heading somewhere. Story helps us to see that the fragments of our lives belong to larger, more complicated arcs and narratives. Stories help us cohere as whole persons, evoking our emotions, our intellects, our bodies, and our wills in the work of pursuing God.

In this sense, story gives us agency. It makes us characters, actors, drivers of the action. Priest and professor Barbara Brown Taylor writes that the meaning we give to what happens in our lives is our final, inviolable freedom. God will never trespass on it. It's up to us to choose the meanings of our days and nights and years and decades. It's up to us to choose the size and shape of the story we'll stake our lives on.

Not all stories are benign. We live in a cultural moment when our choices are both endless and consequential. If we want, we can choose a story about fear and scarcity, a story that demands the policing of borders, the hoarding of resources, and the rejection of all who are different from us. If we want, we can choose a story about doublespeak and deception, a story in which truth no longer matters, our words have no weight or value, and sexy lies have more power than plain authenticity. If we want, we can choose a story about punishment, a story in which our worst mistakes and most shameful moments define and trap us. If we want, we can choose a story about futility—a story that insists we are alone in this universe, abandoned, lost, and forgotten. If we want, we can choose a story about denial—a story that refuses to ask hard questions, avoids all talk of loss and pain, and keeps us wading in the shallows.

Or we can choose a story about God, and God's Son, and God's Spirit, and God's people. A story about grace, forgiveness, love, and resurrection. A story about countless others, our elders in the faith, who, the writer of Hebrews tells us, "confessed that they were strangers and foreigners on the earth," and yet spent their lives "seeking a homeland," "desir[ing] a better country," and wrestling in faith to usher in the reign of God (11:13–16).

Some years ago, my husband, kids, and I got hooked for a few months on a TV series called *Once Upon a Time*. Its premise (at least in Season 1) is that all our favorite fairy tale characters, having been cursed by a powerful Evil Queen, are living in exile in our world—specifically, in a town called Storybrook, in back-woods Maine. But the queen has wiped their memories, and they have no idea who they really are or where they come from. Jiminy Cricket is a psychotherapist. The Blue Fairy is a nun. Snow White is a lonely schoolteacher named Mary Margaret who has no idea that David—the cute guy lying in a coma at the local hospital—is Prince Charming, the love of her life.

It falls to a little boy (of course), to discover the truth, thwart the Evil Queen, and convince the inhabitants of Storybrook that the story they think they're living in is only partial. That there's more. That there's magic.

I think this is our work, too. To remember that the story we're living in is only part of a much bigger story. To keep our eyes open for glimpses of More. To trust that God's Story and ours are intimately connected, even when—especially when—we can't see those connections clearly.

In *Still*, Episcopal priest Lauren Winner recounts a story she heard from a friend. When the friend was twelve years old and preparing for confirmation, she backtracked. She told her father she wasn't sure she could go through with it. She wasn't sure she could believe everything she was supposed to believe, and she didn't want to make a promise of faith she couldn't keep.

Her wise father responded with this: "What you promise when you are confirmed is not that you will believe this forever. What you promise when you are confirmed is that this is the story you will wrestle with forever."

Holocaust survivor and human rights activist Elie Wiesel cites a Hasidic parable in *Gates of the Forest* that ends with the provocative possibility that God made humankind because God loves stories.

The best stories affirm that life is complicated, that easy answers rarely satisfy, and that even the shiniest "happily ever after" endings exact a price. But they also affirm that life isn't random or meaningless. Our participation—our wrestling—matters, because God cherishes this good and sacred story. God, too, leans in with bated breath and asks, "What will happen next?" At great risk and with great love, God has written God's self into the narrative and is forever implicated in the spacious story of faith we inhabit together.

5 | SHE BLOWS WHERE SHE WILLS: SPIRIT

In a 2009 TED Talk titled "The Power of a Single Story," Nigerian novelist Chimamanda Ngozi Adichie argued that "the single story robs people of dignity. It makes our recognition of our equal humanity difficult." It makes one story "become the only story."

At some point in our wrestling out of creed and into story, we must reckon with the problem of the one story. The one telling. The one way of speaking and inhabiting our faith.

My parents' native language of Malayalam is one of India's twenty-two official languages. Though my parents immigrated to the United States when I was an infant, they insisted we speak Malayalam at home, so I grew up bilingual.

I also grew up with a divided and defensive sense of identity. *We* (brown people) were Indian and spoke Malayalam, while *they* (white people) were American and spoke only English. As immigrants who were determined to make America our home, *we* would cross the great divide and master English, too, but the linguistic traffic would never flow in the opposite direction. After all, I had never met an American who'd even heard of my language—this despite the fact that close to forty million people on the planet speak it. "What's it called again?" my friends would ask when I sounded out the four-syllable palindrome.

Or—worse—"Wait, I don't get it. I thought Indians speak Hindu."

I must have been nine or ten years old when my aunt and uncle called our extended family together one weekend for a "surprise." When all thirty of us were packed into the living room, my uncle introduced a guest—a blond-haired, blue-eyed woman in her thirties named Sarah. He explained only that Sarah had spent a few childhood years in Delhi, where her parents worked as journalists, and that her family had vacationed occasionally in Kerala. He then handed things over to her.

It's hard to do justice to what happened next. Basically, thirty brown jaws crashed to the carpet when Sarah nodded to my uncle, smiled warmly at us, and said, *"Namaskaram, ningalay ellavarayum kandathil ennicku santhosham ondu."* ("Hello, I'm so happy to meet all of you.")

Over the next twenty minutes, while we gawked and gaped, Sarah told us her story in careful but perfectly convincing Malayalam. Those childhood trips to Kerala had fascinated her, she said—so much so that she moved to South India after college and immersed herself in the language and culture. "It was very hard," she admitted. "Learning the script, forming such new sounds—annoying people with my mistakes. But I'm so glad I did."

Over dinner, she went on to explain how much her Kerala immersion changed her. "I didn't realize before how limited my own perceptions were. My ideas about humor, about art, about God. I didn't know how many things were unsayable in a single language."

I thought about Sarah for a long time after that evening because her visit altered my understanding of language, word, story, and belief. Something became possible for the first time: an alliance, a bridging, a new kind of empathy and friendship. When my family experienced the unprecedented pleasure of hearing "an American" speak our language, we realized that the many distances separating "us" from "them" were not, in fact, uncrossable. Sarah, the stranger, had taken a risk, made herself vulnerable, and entered our world. She had interrupted the single story, and in doing so, she had rendered *us* less strange. Less alien. Less other.

She had also offered us a crucial challenge: it would no longer be possible, in the light of her generosity, to hang onto our self-protective narratives about identity. She had bulldozed her way through that barrier, and only a massive act of denial on our part would reerect it.

For me, another event that breaks barriers in the same way is Pentecost: the birthday of the church. In the Pentecost story Luke narrates in the book of Acts, the Holy Spirit descends on one hundred twenty believers in Jerusalem. The Spirit empowers them to testify to God's great deeds, emboldens the apostle Peter to preach to a bewildered crowd of Jewish skeptics, and draws three thousand converts to Christianity in a single day.

It's a birthday story like no other, full of wild details that challenge the imagination. Tongues of fire. Rushing winds. Accusations of drunkenness. Mass conversion. To put it bluntly: God shows up fifty days after Jesus's resurrection and throws the world a party.

75

But God does more than that at Pentecost. I believe God gives the early believers a clear and startling picture of what Christ's body on earth should look like. God reveals a vision and a dream for the church—a dream of many stories, many tellings, many rooms.

"All of them were filled with the Holy Spirit," Luke writes, "and began to speak in other languages, as the Spirit gave them ability. . . . At this sound the crowd gathered and was bewildered, because each one heard them speaking in the native language of each" (Acts 2:4, 6).

Christians sometimes speak of Pentecost as the reversal of the tower of Babel, the Genesis story in which God divides and scatters human communities by multiplying their languages. But in fact, Pentecost doesn't reverse Babel; it perfects and blesses it. When the Holy Spirit comes upon the disciples, she doesn't restore humanity to a common language and a single story; the Spirit declares all languages holy and equally worthy of God's stories. The Spirit weaves diversity, multivocality, and inclusiveness into the very fabric of the church.

Those of us who speak more than one language might be the best equipped to grasp the import of this divine declaration, this miraculous weaving. We understand intuitively that a language holds far more than the sum of its grammar, vocabulary, and syntax. Languages carry the full weight of their respective cultures, histories, psychologies, and spiritualities. To speak one language as opposed to another is to orient oneself differently in the world: to see differently, hear differently, process and punctuate reality differently. There is no such thing as a perfect translation.

If this is true, then what does it mean that the Holy Spirit empowers the first Christians to speak in an unmatched diversity of languages? Perhaps God is saying that the church needs to honor the boundless variety and creativity of human voices. Not because multiculturalism is progressive and fashionable, or because the church is a "politically correct" institution, but because God's deeds themselves demand such diverse tellings. Could it be that there is no single language, story, creed, or mother tongue on earth that can fully capture the spaciousness and the hospitality of God?

Here's a detail I cherish about the Pentecost story: When the disciples and their friends begin to speak in foreign languages, the crowds gathered outside their meeting place understand them. And this *fact* of their comprehension is what confuses them.

They're not confused by the message itself; the message comes through with perfect clarity in their respective languages. What the crowds find baffling is that God condescends to speak to them in their own mother tongues. That God welcomes them so intimately, with words and expressions hearkening back to their birthplaces, their childhoods, their beloved cities, countries, and cultures of origin. They find this stunning, the idea that God essentially says: "This Spirit-drenched place, this fledgling church, this new body of Christ, is *yours*. You don't have to feel like outsiders here; we speak your language, too. Come in. Come in and feel at home."

Christians place great stock in language. In *words*. Like our Jewish and Muslim siblings, we are People of the Book. We love the creation stories of Genesis, in which God births the very cosmos into existence by speaking: "And God *said*." "In the beginning was the Word," we read in John's dazzling poem about the incarnate Christ. On Sunday mornings, we profess our faith in the languages of liturgy, creed, prayer, and music. In short, we believe that language has power. Words make worlds—and unmake them, too.

To attempt one language as opposed to another is to make oneself a learner, a servant, a supplicant. To speak across barriers of race, ethnicity, gender, religion, culture, denomination, or politics is to challenge stereotype and risk ridicule. It is a brave and disorienting act.

Whether we like it or not, this is what the Holy Spirit required of Christ's frightened disciples on the birthday of the church. They were asked to stop huddling in sameness and safety. To throw open their windows and doors. To feel the pressure of God's hand against their backs, pour themselves into the streets, and speak. When the Holy Spirit arrived, the single story became impossible.

In the end, God's tongues of fire required surrender on both sides. Those who spoke had to brave languages outside of their comfort zones. They had to risk vulnerability in the face of difference, and do so with no guarantee of welcome. They had to trust that no matter how awkward, inadequate, or silly they felt, the words bubbling up inside of them—new, strange, and scary ones—were nevertheless *essential* words. They were words precisely ordained for the time and place they occupied.

Meanwhile, the crowds who listened had to take risks as well. They had to suspend disbelief, drop their cherished defenses, and opt for wonder instead of contempt. They had to widen their creeds and their circles and welcome strangers with odd accents into their midst.

Not all of them managed it. Some sneered because they couldn't bear to be bewildered, to have their neat categories of belonging and exclusion explode in their faces. Instead, like their ancestors at Babel, who scattered at the first sign of difference, they retreated into the well-worn narrative of denial: "Nothing new is happening here. This isn't God. These are blubbering idiots who've had too much to drink."

But even in that atmosphere of suspicion and cynicism, some people spoke, and some people listened, and into those astonishing exchanges, God breathed fresh life.

Something happens when we resist the single story. Something happens when we speak each other's languages, be they cultural, political, racial, theological, or liturgical. We experience the limits of our own perspectives. We learn curiosity. We discover that God's "deeds of power" (Acts 2:11) are far too nuanced for a single tongue, a single fluency. And we enter into a world where rich particularity opens out into a fuller, roomier community.

Right now, we live in a world where words have become toxic, where the languages of our cherished "isms" threaten to divide and destroy us. What languages do we need to speak that we've never spoken before? Where does the fire need to fall, to burn away all that hinders us from being bearers of good news in a dark time? If we don't learn the art of speaking each other's languages and hearing each other's stories, we'll burn ourselves down to ash.

Because here's the thing: No matter how passionately I disagree with your opinions, creeds, doctrines, or beliefs, I cannot disagree with your *story*. Once I have learned to hear and speak your story in the words that matter most to you, then I have stakes I never had before. I can no longer flourish at your expense. I can no longer stand over you in condemnation. I can no longer abandon you as an "other" I need not care about.

Bold openness is what the Holy Spirit required of Christ's frightened disciples on the birthday of the church. Bold openness is what we're called to now. In so many languages, through so many stories, at the heart of all the eloquent creeds we profess, the Spirit is sending us out the door with a dizzying array of stories to share. "Speak, scatter, listen, and learn," the Spirit says in a thousand beautiful mother tongues. "You are on fire."

———

But given Christianity's complicated and sometimes sordid history, what does it mean to practice such bold openness? I love the roomy spiritual house God invites us to inhabit, but I can't insist that others enter it. I don't want to repeat the sins of cultural and religious colonialism; Christians don't hold the global monopoly on spiritual meaning, wisdom, or truth. Moreover, I have no desire to be false in my relationships, feigning love in order to manipulate others into believing as I do.

One way out of this dilemma—a popular way these days—is to insist that all spiritual paths are ultimately the same, that the apparent differences between faiths are surface-level differences only, since all paths lead up to the same mountaintop. I'm wary of this "solution," because it posits a bird's-eye view that I have no right to claim. Why do I think I can see the whole mountain while all the good people trekking up their various winding paths cannot? Who put me on the summit?

The image of myriad, disconnected hikers laboring up a rocky mountain also strikes me as a profoundly lonely and solipsistic one, especially when I hold it up to the vivid imagery of Pentecost. When the Holy Spirit came, people crossed paths. They *talked*. They shared stories. They asked questions. They built sturdy, dependable bridges across their cherished mother tongues.

In short, they dared to listen and learn from each other. They dared to discern truth in community.

I wonder if a humble and respectful way forward for us is to honor religious differences as genuine, meaningful, and consequential. Yes, this is vastly harder than pretending that the differences don't exist or matter. But this braver way offers us an invitation to actually engage the civilizational questions that religions are about—questions about what truly constitutes liberation, transformation, hope, and healing, not for a select few but for all.

Whenever the prospect of sharing my faith story daunts me, I try to remember that when Jesus announced his good news, he was offering an oppressed people a subversive alternative to the cruel dehumanization of empire. Likewise, my earliest Christian ancestors lived and died in the hope of offering the world an invitation to radical, life-changing love. Love grounded in Jesus's death and resurrection, enlivened and manifested in sacred community. In other words, the gospel from its inception was newsworthy because it was deeply *good*. So at what point does our silence become offensive in its own right—offensive as in withholding, ungenerous, inhospitable?

Jesus's bold openness never involved manipulation or coercion. His way was to listen, to ask questions, to tell stories, and to let folks walk away with what they'd seen and heard. The invitation to "come and see" was always open. But so was the freedom to doubt, question, and disagree. Jesus didn't lead with the arrogant assumption that he was *bringing* God anywhere, but rather with the deep trust that God's Spirit was already way out ahead of him, blowing where she willed, as mysterious as the wind.

I am the heir of a sacred story St. Thomas chose to share across formidable borders. And yes, over the centuries that followed his visit to India, waves of missionaries, preachers, evangelists—and colonizers—swept into my parents' home country, sharing the gospel, distorting the gospel, disgracing the gospel, and upholding the gospel. By turns.

There are aspects of this history that rightfully infuriate me, that break my heart, that cause me to question the whole business of sharing stories of faith. Yet I still believe that somehow, across the years and despite human folly, God's good news remained good. Even amid the shadows, it brought healing, hope, and transformation to my ancestors. The Spirit blew where she would, and new life followed in her wake.

In the church I attend now in northern California, we pray each Sunday for the global church. But before we do, we confess and repent. We ask God to keep us ever mindful "of the sins of colonial conquest" that have accompanied the worldwide spread of the Christian story. We acknowledge the historic and catastrophic sins Christians have committed, and we ask forgiveness for the sins committed on our behalf.

But then we make a turn toward gratitude and hope. We ask "for the grace to receive the gifts our global communion offers us."

We do this because it *is* possible, with God's help, to hold the nuance of the One Story and the many stories. To find ways to speak the sins and the gifts, the wounds and the graces. If the wild and fiery Spirit of God can birth new life in the midst of all our human diversity, beauty, and brokenness, we can find the courage to tell her story.

6 | GETTING SAVED: SIN

Growing up, I spent an inordinate amount of time doing two things: obsessing over sin and begging for salvation. Well into my high school years, I was a magnet for revival songs, altar calls, and come-to-Jesus sermons. I cried every time I heard the penitential hymn "Just as I Am." In Sunday school, and in the church pews, and by my bed with an NIV Children's Bible propped open on a throw pillow, I begged Jesus again and again to forgive my sins, come into my heart, and clean house. I got saved compulsively.

The front page of that old Bible still documents my many salvations: June 1, 1981. January 5, 1983. March 24, 1984. April 7, 1987. Easter Sunday 1988. Most of the dates are crossed out, signifying salvations that, for whatever reason, didn't stick and required a do-over.

I kept detailed journals as a kid, so I have records of the sins that tormented me: "God, I threw my broccoli under my brother's chair at dinner, so Dad would think he dropped it." "God, I snuck *Anne of Green Gables* into my Bible and read it during church." "God, I didn't finish my math homework, so I lost it on purpose."

As I got older, the entries changed, becoming less about specific actions and more about the person I feared I was becoming: "God, I can't be the good Indian daughter I'm supposed to be."

"God, I don't know how to trust you when I'm scared all the time." "God, I keep trying to be close to you, but I don't feel you at all." "God, I'm always ashamed. God, who I am is not okay."

When I read these later entries now, I see all the ways in which I conflated sin with cultural identity and loyalty. To be "pure" was to be purely Indian as my faith community defined it. To be "sinful" was to be culturally hybrid or just plain confused.

The irony is that the version of Christianity my family practiced in my childhood was not indigenous; it was whitewashed. Christianity had belonged to my ancestors for centuries, yes. But the particular flavor we practiced in my childhood came to us by way of white Pentecostal and Brethren missionaries who went to India in the 1930s, 1940s, and 1950s and preached a Puritan-style austerity as essential to Christian living. I grew up with an Indianness that was a sad shell of itself.

In practice, this meant I didn't celebrate or even know about any South Asian holidays or festivals. Until I met non-Christian Indians in college, I had no idea what Diwali was. Or Onam. Or Holi. Or Eid al-Fitr or Muharram.

In my Indian Christian family, these celebrations were considered pagan and therefore taboo. Even to educate myself about them was to trespass into sinfulness. Plain clothes, plain worship. No dancing, no jewelry, no pageantry, no ecumenical festivals, celebrations, or collaborations. In short, no *Indianness*. I was well into adulthood before I learned to recast this "purity" as the cultural colonialism it was.

In his thought-provoking book *The Christian Imagination: Theology and the Origins of Race*, Willie James Jennings examines the intersections of Christianity, colonization, cultural imperialism, and race to reveal just how much damage white, Western

Christianity has wreaked around the world. Why, he asks, has Christianity—a religion supposedly rooted in neighborly love— failed so often to bridge cultural gaps and dismantle segregation? What would it look like to embrace a truly Christlike vision of deep joining rather than deep division?

For an immigrant kid like me, these questions weren't academic; they were personal and urgent. Who decided that *faithful* and *Western* should be synonyms? That "sinfulness" was brown-skinned? I grew up having no idea that God might be okay with "pagan" things like bangles, henna, and bindis.

But as a preteen and teenager, I didn't have a language or context for any of this. I considered the "failures" I listed in my cloth-bound notebooks truly egregious, and as I jotted them down night after night, I prayed hard, willing my own redemption. I pictured my sinfulness as a towering wall separating me from a holy God who couldn't tolerate my depravity. My job was to push, pummel, and pound the wall until it crumbled, allowing God to relent and return.

Those were exhausting years, spent striving for God's love and acceptance. For all my talk of God's power, I lived in deep and abiding fear of my own. My capacity to sin seemed outsized, past the point of no return, and at times I lost all hope of salvation.

It didn't help that I was a preacher's kid—up front and visible, with a keen sense that I needed to be "a good example" for my father's congregants. The shadow side of my parents' wonderfully tight-knit immigrant community was its strict honor-shame ethos. Though my battles over sin felt very personal, the culture I lived in was collectivist; we were all connected, and even our tiniest choices rippled through the community in ever-widening arcs. Appearances mattered. Reputation mattered. Social capital mattered.

This meant that the moral stakes were high. As I saw it, God and I were locked in a fierce two-person play before a highly attentive audience. "Sin" was what I did and who I was. "Salvation" was an elusive prize I had to earn. Life on this harshly lit stage was small, insular, and cramped: there was God, there was me, and there was the concrete wall that separated us. That was the entire play. Nothing else.

As soon as they leave home or reach adulthood, kids who have grown up in conservative Christian communities like mine often throw off the conceptual weight that both "sin" and "salvation" carry. I understand; it's a reasonable response. It's terrible to feel that what God desires most is our remorse. That the only way to win God's heart is to feel wretched about my own.

It's also difficult to take seriously the small, cloistered world of evangelical sin once we step outside of it. By the time I left home for college, I could no longer believe that drinking alcohol, having sex before marriage, and wearing skinny jeans were egregious evils while abusing our planet, shunning our gay neighbors, and denying the consequences of systemic racism were not.

I also grew weary of repenting for things I could no longer view as sinful: My doubts and questions about Christianity. My struggles with depression and anxiety. My rage against the patriarchy's hold on my life and the church. The secret desires I harbored to explore India's more colorful and festive traditions, holidays, and artistic offerings—the ones my austere Christian family considered pagan. The ambivalence and shame I felt about my brown-skinned, female body in predominantly white spaces. My inability to fit that body into either cultural mold—Indian or American—that my faith communities considered sacrosanct.

At the same time, as I moved out into a wider and more complicated world, I decided that I needed a roomier understanding of sin. Whatever "living in sin" meant (a phrase I heard often in sermons), it had to encompass something far broader and deeper than an individual human being living with the consequences of their own moral failure. I couldn't deny that beauty was everywhere. But *brokenness* was everywhere, too, and very often, that brokenness had little to do with personal purity or morality. It was more elemental than volitional—a toxin in the air, a wrongness in the water. In the people I met, worked with, and loved, I sensed a deep longing for the just, the meaningful, and the good. And yet I also sensed *something* that warred incessantly against those longings. Undermining them. Twisting them. Distorting them.

Whatever sin was, I could no longer believe that it resided in the guilt-ridden journal entries of my childhood. In Scripture, sin is not primarily about us making mistakes, or choosing poorly, or missing the mark, or taking wrong turns. Sin is the broken state of our world, the hard reality of our universe, the layered zeitgeist of human life. To confess that we "live in sin" is not simply to confess private moral failings. It is to name something universal and cosmic that wars so insidiously within us, between us, and around us that it twists and deforms our souls and our societies.

In this sense, plenty of people—completely apart from any concept of moral failure—are still "living in sin": that is, living with the painful and oppressive consequences of having a certain skin color, or nationality, or ethnicity, or sexual orientation, or gender, or neurochemistry, or family history, or zip code.

In time, I moved into Christian circles quite different from the ones in which I'd grown up. And I learned that conservative evangelical baggage isn't the only background that leads to distrusting the "s" words. Progressive Christians who have never been connected to evangelicalism distrust the church's focus on sin and salvation, too. To mainline Christian ears, *sin* is often considered an intolerant, obsolete word soaked in guilt, shame, punishment, and hellfire. Focusing on sin jerks us away from God, progressives say, instead of drawing us more deeply into God's arms. It cuts against the grain of our optimism about human potential and perfectibility. In their view, the core truth of our identities isn't original sin. It's original blessing.

In a progressive context, evangelical conceptions of *salvation* often grate against the ear, too. They sound selfish, narcissistic, and even lazy. If our problems as a species are primarily political, socioeconomic, and cultural, then why linger over remorse and repentance? Shouldn't we just hit the streets and resist injustice in hands-on ways? Isn't it a cop-out, an abdication of responsibility, to wait for Jesus to do the saving? He has already shown us the revolutionary love the world needs. Now we just have to go out and practice it.

I appreciate the appeal of this perspective, and I wholeheartedly agree that the work of justice *is* our work. But as I've shuttled between conservative and progressive Christian traditions, I've come to see how desperately we still need the "s" words. We *need* a robust understanding of sin's insidious reach and power, one that recognizes evil as a malevolent force we can't defeat by our good intentions or our willpower.

And we need a vision of salvation that's equally robust. In the New Testament, both Jesus and St. Paul describe sin as enslavement (John 8:34; Romans 6:17), implying that humanity needs an emancipator. We are bound by chains we'll never break on our own.

In other words, we need to embrace a vision of the "s" words that is both cosmic and intimate: a vision that empowers us to act and at the same time recognizes our inability to save ourselves. We cannot love our way into our own liberation; we need the cruciform love of Christ to course through us. We need a Savior who will reshape and reform the labyrinthine realms of our sinful hearts so that we can participate in God's global work of healing and transformation. The only reason we can "work out [our] own salvation," as St. Paul puts it (Philippians 2:12), is because God is already working God's salvation in us.

If God's house is truly big enough to hold us in all our complexity, then it's big enough to hold the "s" words too. Rightly understood, *sin* and *salvation* are precisely the roomy, expansive words we need to ground our vocations as Christ's hands and feet in a pain-filled world. Walking away from these core tenets of our faith grants us no more freedom, spaciousness, resilience, or hope than my anxious childhood sprints to the altar.

———

A few years ago, in the wake of George Floyd's murder and the nationwide protests that followed, my then-teenage son asked me this: "How is Christianity different from progressivism? What does being a Christian offer you that being a good person— committed to equality and justice and compassion—does not?"

The question merited all sorts of answers, and at the time, I gave my son several. Being a Christian gives me hope, I told him. Hope for this life and for the life to come. Being a Christian assures me that I am known and loved by a generous, self-giving God. Being a Christian helps me remember that I'm not alone when I suffer; I'm accompanied by Jesus, who willingly experienced pain, loss, betrayal, and death in solidarity with his fellow humans. Being a Christian reminds me that I live in a created world—a world that is sacred and meaningful, shot through with God's artistry. Being a Christian grants me the gift of the incarnation: the promise that our bodies are sacred, and that all the stuff of this world—skin, bone, earth, water, star, stone, rose, sparrow—matters to God. Being a Christian gives me a distinct sense of purpose and vocation—to do justice, and love mercy, and practice humility before God and God's people.

I liked these answers when I offered them, and I like them still. They feel solid and true. But looking back, I wish I'd said more, because the answers I gave my son were incomplete. They skip over Christianity's sharper edge—the hard, honest edge that distinguishes the life of faith from generic goodness or niceness.

In fact, it's the very concept of niceness that an honest engagement with faith must call into question. What does being a Christian give me that being a "good person" does not? It gives me sinfulness. Or rather Sinfulness, with a capital S. It gives me a truth that cuts before it heals, the truth that Sin is not a six-year-old throwing broccoli under the dining table, or a teenager wrestling with her parents over her cultural identity, or a college student having a beer. Sin is a deadly, malevolent force that wars against creation. It's a power that seeks to diminish, distort, and destroy our dignity as beloved children of God. It's not primarily an act or an inclination. It's a prison cell I can't escape on my own.

I think we flinch away from conversations about sin because we conceptualize it in ways that aren't faithful to Scripture or to the radical nature of the gospel. We assume that the "s" words can only ever impose burdens of guilt and shame on our lives, trapping us in vicious cycles of remorse and repentance from which there's no escape.

But what if the biblical language of Sin and Salvation is actually about offering us a way *out* of those cycles? What if Sin's stage is far wider than anything I conceived of as a young person, locked as I was in my little drama with God? And what if Salvation's scale is infinite in both directions, encompassing the intimately personal *and* the mind-bogglingly universal?

In one of his most famous passages in Romans, St. Paul describes sin as an enslavement that frustrates and bewilders him: "I do not understand my own actions. For I do not do what I want, but I do the very thing I hate. . . . For I delight in the law of God in my inmost self, but I see in my members another law at war with the law of my mind, making me captive to the law of sin that dwells in my members. Wretched man that I am! Who will rescue me from this body of death?" (Romans 7:15, 22–24).

For Paul, sin management isn't about hard work and brute willpower; it's not a matter of management at all. It's a battle for his very life, a battle that he sees and experiences as if from the outside, looking in: "I see in my members another law at war with the law of my mind." His desire for God, his delight in God, his commitment to God—these are vibrant and beautiful, but they're not enough. He's a "captive" who needs a deliverer.

In other words, sin for Paul is an aggressive and powerful force that enslaves us even when we're convinced of our own decency and piety. It can—and does!—sit right alongside our passionate efforts to love and obey God.

I know that describing sin as a "force" can sound unnecessarily spooky and supernatural. After all, aren't we more enlightened now? Why resurrect the ancient language of spirits, demons, and devils to describe what's wrong with our world? Do we really need to conjure a horned figure with a tail and a pitchfork who tempts us in the night?

No, we don't. What we do need is to take seriously the biblical idea that evil is powerfully oppositional. It functions as an adversary (a *satan*, in Hebrew), thwarting God's purposes for us and for all of creation. In other words, we need to understand that we can take the mythological language of Scripture to heart without literalizing it. It *is* possible to bring our twenty-first-century sensibilities to bear on the Bible's depiction of sin and evil—and still find its witness sturdy and true.

For me, holding this nuance, this both-and, is the only way I can make sense of the world when I wake up each morning and read the headlines. Whether we're talking about our collective inertia and apathy in response to gun violence, or our inability to take the catastrophic nature of climate change seriously, or our complacency in the face of ongoing racial injustice, or our tepid responses to rape culture: We are up against something ominous, vicious, and real, something that works in the spaces above, below, and between us. Something that includes but also exceeds our small, private choices—and even our individual capacities to *make* those choices.

In his exhaustive historical study, *A Secular Age*, philosopher Charles Taylor argues that in contemporary Western culture, we no longer have available to us the bulwarks that made faith easier in previous eras. We no longer view the natural world as testimony; we view it through the lens of science. The phrase "acts of God" has become a dead metaphor.

We no longer live in societies where God is deeply implicated in civic life—where religious ritual and worship underlie our social, political, educational, and economic activities. For good reasons, we've erected walls of separation between religion and state. It's not theocracy we need; it's a roomier and more generous vision of the sacred and the mysterious in our everyday lives.

We no longer live in an enchanted world, Taylor argues—a world in which spirits, demons, and moral forces are believed to play active roles in human destinies. Though we indulge our children in these fantastical beliefs when they're young, we fully expect them to shed their fantasies before adulthood. In short, we no longer live in a world where "fullness"—that numinous sense of "more," of wonder, of awe, of profound meaning and significance—is believed to exist.

And yet there's a reason the Gospel writers whose testimonies we value so highly describe Jesus's forty days in the wilderness as a prolonged encounter with Satan. There's a reason Jesus develops a reputation as a skilled and committed exorcist. There's a reason he asks his disciples to take up the ministry of exorcism, too. There's a reason Jesus's rebuke to hotheaded Peter in Matthew 16 is eerily metaphysical: "Get behind me, Satan!" (v. 23).

In his book *Reviving Old Scratch*, Richard Beck articulates a theology of spiritual warfare for modern Christians. In describing the satan-adversary as "real," he says the following:

> I'd love to have a Christianity full of rainbows and daisies, full of love and inclusion. But there are forces working against love and inclusion in the world, and some of those forces are at work in my own heart and mind. We call those forces *hate* and *exclusion*, to say nothing about everything else that is tearing the world to shreds, pushing the loving and gracious rule of God out of the world.
>
> Hate is the satan of love.
> Exclusion is the satan of inclusion.
> War is the satan of peace.
> Oppression is the satan of justice.
> Tearing down is the satan of building up.
> Competition is the satan of cooperation.
> Revenge is the satan of mercy.
> Harm is the satan of care.
> Hostility is the satan of reconciliation.
> There is a satan to the kingdom of God.

If we disenchant sin, Beck writes—if we reject "satan" or "the adversary" as a viable theological category—we will sooner or later demonize each other. Instead of directing our indignation, bewilderment, sorrow, and anger toward the Sin that binds all of us, we'll choose scapegoats to condemn and despise. We'll draw sharp distinctions between our own goodness and someone else's badness, and we'll fail to recognize that we're all in the same boat together, sinking. We'll mistake genuine human needs, hopes, and hungers—for intimacy, for belonging, for creative expression, for ethnic and cultural integrity—as sinfulness.

I wish a robust theology of Sin wasn't such a hard sell. I wish we could embrace Christianity's "s" words as liberating, because they are. "Abandoning the language of sin will not make sin go away," theologian Barbara Brown Taylor writes. "Human beings will continue to experience alienation, deformation, damnation and death no matter what we call them. Abandoning the language will simply leave us speechless before them, and increase our denial of their presence in our lives. Ironically, it will also weaken the language of grace, since the full impact of forgiveness cannot be felt apart from the full impact of what has been forgiven."

Embracing Paul's take on sin gives us a viable place to begin, a roomy place to stand. It tells us the truth, which is that we are both beautiful and broken, made in God's divine image but bound by something that works against our efforts to be good and do good. To use the word *sin* is to insist on something more profound and more clarifying than to say, "I make mistakes" or "I have issues." To use the word *sin* is to understand that we need Jesus to be more than a good role model, life coach, or mentor. We need Jesus to save us—to break an ancient and malevolent power we cannot break by ourselves. To use the word *sin* is to confess, as Paul does, that we are "wretched" in the face of Sin's power and lost without the cross.

Lutheran pastor Nadia Bolz-Weber puts it this way: "No one is climbing the spiritual ladder. We don't continually improve until we are so spiritual we no longer need God. We die and are made new, but that's different from spiritual self-improvement.

We are simultaneously sinner and saint, 100 percent of both, all the time."

A roomier understanding of sin requires an equally roomy vision of salvation. But when I think back over the anxious years I spent begging God to save me, *roominess* is not the word that comes to mind. I remember my deep fear of estrangement, and of losing God's favor and affection. I remember believing that salvation is fundamentally transactional: if I do A, God will do B. If I sign on the dotted line, I'll get a clean slate and God will like me.

What I don't remember is a compelling vision of a "saved" life that might empower me to become an active agent of God's salvific work in the world I inhabit. Salvation was an ending, not a beginning. A culmination, after which I could just sit tight and bask in my eternal security. Not a provocation. Not a firm, loving push out the door.

Nor do I remember salvation as holistic, inclusive, and global. The good news, as I understood it, centered exclusively on the forgiveness of sins for a small subsection of humanity— the few who prayed the "sinner's prayer" and accepted Jesus into their hearts as their personal Savior. Jesus's death on the cross was an effective antidote for those people's individual moral failures, but it had little to offer everyone else: the people who couldn't make sense out of the sinner's prayer, the people who earnestly sought the sacred in other faith traditions, the people whose "bad news" was more about sorrow, fear, pain, trauma, loneliness, oppression, abuse, addiction, poverty, or loss than wrongdoing.

Moreover, the crucified Christ I grew up venerating couldn't help the more-than-human world in *its* vast and heartbreaking brokenness. The world of polluted oceans, starving polar bears, scorched sequoias, and endangered butterflies. Where was the good news for God's groaning creation—the streams, mountains, cliffs, and canyons God once so lovingly spoke into being?

To imagine a roomier salvation is not to minimize our need for personal forgiveness or to abandon our hope in heaven. Rather, it is to embrace salvation in the most comprehensive sense: as wholeness, transformation, liberation, and healing. A truly efficacious "salve" for everything that ails God's world: our failures and their pernicious effects, yes, but also our wounds, our hungers, our thirsts, our aches, our losses, our terrors, our traumas, our deaths.

In the Hebrew Bible, salvation arrives in varied and astonishing guises. It offers companionship to the lonely. It provides manna for the hungry and clothing for the naked. It grants reprieve to the murderer, freedom for the enslaved, and justice for the oppressed. Salvation includes babies for the barren. Affection for the abandoned. Guidance for the lost. Homelands for the itinerant. And return for the exile.

Likewise in the Gospels, salvation encompasses everything from wine for a wedding, to bread for the hungry, to cures for the sick, to companionship for the bereaved, to wisdom for the foolish, to faith for the doubtful, to liberation for the demon-possessed, to community for the ostracized, to love for the unlovable, to honor for the shamed, to resurrection for the dead.

Every one of these "salvations" comes from God: God promises, God initiates, God perseveres, and God completes what God begins. No one in Scripture saves themselves. And yet all are invited into the work of salvation as fellow crossbearers with Jesus so that, through God's love incarnated in us, God's salvation can heal and transform the world.

———————

In the Gospel of Luke, Jesus describes humanity as "children sitting in the marketplace" and calling to each other with songs that no one understands (7:32). When they sing happy songs, he says, no one dances. When they play dirges, no one mourns. When John the Baptizer preaches an austere message of remorse and repentance, his listeners say he's demon-possessed. When Jesus comes along, eating and drinking around a common table, his listeners call him a glutton and a drunkard.

Jesus's apt description suggests that when we try to contend with good and evil all by ourselves, we routinely miss what matters. We don't know when to dance, when to mourn, when to repent, when to celebrate. We claim to be wise and discerning, but we don't recognize the divine work of salvation when we encounter it. God is always too much or too little for us, too severe or too generous, too demanding or too provocative. On our own, we have little capacity to discern what is good and right and holy and true. "When I want to do what is good," Paul writes, "evil lies close at hand" (Romans 7:21).

So what hope do we have? Who will rescue us from what Paul calls "these bodies of death"?

Jesus concludes his parable of the children in the marketplace, in Matthew 11:28–30, with some of the most comforting words in the New Testament: "Come to me, all you that are weary and are carrying heavy burdens, and I will give you rest.

Take my yoke upon you, and learn from me; for I am gentle and humble in heart, and you will find rest for your souls. For my yoke is easy, and my burden is light."

When I'm tempted to shun the "s" words—when I fear that they're too toxic, intolerant, or obsolete for the world I live in—I remember Jesus's beautiful, generous, whole-life invitation. I remember that he makes it not to the self-sufficient and the self-righteous, but to the weary and the burdened. He makes that invitation not only to those requiring forgiveness but also to all who are exhausted, overworked, overwhelmed, or oppressed. To all who "live in sin"—which is every single one of us, human and more-than-human—salvation comes as transformation, possibility, hope, refuge, and *rest*. Rest from evil in all its guises. Rest from every kind of hopelessness and death. Rest from the wrongs we do and the wrongs done to us. Rest from the shame we've inherited ourselves and inflicted on others. Rest for those like St. Paul, who know that they're bound by forces too terrible to wield or manage on their own.

But what about heaven?

I can hear the question rising up from my past, from my own childhood self perched on her bed, begging to be saved. It's also the first question I hear when I talk to people about the importance of salvation here and now, here on earth as it is.

Growing up, many of us learned that the number one reason to "get saved" was to go to heaven. I spent years embracing a "pie-in-the-sky" theology: the teaching that this earth is not our home and therefore not our concern. As I got older, I noticed the toxic apathy and poor stewardship that emerge from this kind of overemphasis on the hereafter. Why bother fighting pollution, climate change, or species loss if the planet is doomed to burn anyway? Why bother addressing any injustice that plagues humanity if the earth is just a giant waiting room for heaven?

I also saw how manipulative and traumatic life-after-death preaching can be in its more passionate iterations. I remember cringing at vivid descriptions of hellfire and horrible descriptions of God as cruel, stingy, and vindictive.

And yet. I still believe that a truly roomy Christianity must include an unapologetic vision of heaven. I believe that the historic creed I profess with countless other Christians on Sunday mornings tells me something essential and true: we believe in "the resurrection of the dead and the life of the world to come." If we abandon this belief, we'll do so to our impoverishment and our peril.

Why do I feel this way? Well, at the time of this writing, we are almost four years into a global pandemic. Alongside everything that Covid-19 has taken from us and our loved ones, we live in a world marred by too many mass shootings to count, daily headlines of war, a rapidly worsening climate, increasing economic inequality, ongoing racist violence, and a second global pandemic of mental illness and anguish.

In the face of all this, I need to know that a better world is not just possible but assured. I need to trust that God's salvation encompasses not only those of us who enjoy fairly comfortable lives here on earth but also those who will not experience the salvific love, vindication, healing, and justice of God in this life.

In other words, I believe in heaven because I believe in God's salvation for the children who have died and will die in elementary school classrooms because the United States worships guns. For the millions around the world who died of the coronavirus before vaccines were developed. For Black, brown, Indigenous, gay, and transgender Americans who live in perpetual fear of violence and recrimination on our streets. For the young people who live under the shadow of mental illnesses that modern medicine can't yet alleviate. For casualties of war around the world. For people in chronic pain. For people who, for whatever reason, experience life on this earth as burdensome, lonely, terrifying, or hopeless.

For all these people, I need to know that love, hope, and justice are secured by the Christ who died for them, too. I need to know that, while we have every obligation to alleviate suffering in this world, the salvation of God's precious children does not, finally, depend upon our clumsy efforts. That the pain of human life matters infinitely to God—so much so that God's working out of healing, equity, reconciliation, and justice will not end when a human being draws their final breath on this planet. That somehow, somewhere, someday, God will wipe every tear from every eye.

The truth is, millions of people will spend the whole of their earthly lives fighting without respite against forces that diminish them. Our toxic positivity notwithstanding, *some things will be lost.* For me, the hope of heaven is the guarantee that these beloved children of God—the least of these we fail to see—will eventually experience God's love and justice too. If not, then what does God's justice mean?

I no longer worry that a robust belief in heaven will lead to a lazy escapism. We are capable of more nuance than this. We can hold the both-and of heaven *and* earth, faith *and* works, trust in the hereafter *and* active engagement now.

I worry about the opposite: if Christians lose our belief in the resurrection of the dead and the life of the world to come, we will also lose the ferocity of our hope, the holy restlessness that leads us to action, the commitment to justice that fuels our prophetic lament, solidarity, resilience, and courage. After all, how will we pray for God's kingdom to come, and how will we credibly usher in that kingdom in whatever small ways we can here and now, if we don't believe in its ultimate fulfillment?

Sometimes I wonder if the church's witness is failing because we don't know how to translate a theology of heaven for the times in which we live. Our culture's images of heaven are so saccharine, so sentimental, so boring. What would it be like to move beyond clouds, harps, and chubby baby angels? To hold out the possibility of actual peace, reconciliation, and abundance for all?

When the writers of Scripture describe God's kingdom, they use language that's far more radical than the language of Hallmark greeting cards. In Isaiah 11:6–9, the prophet describes nothing less than the reordering of creation into a peaceable kingdom:

The wolf shall live with the lamb,
   the leopard shall lie down with the kid,
   the calf and the lion and the fatling together;
   and a little child shall lead them.
The cow and the bear shall graze;
   their young shall lie down together;
   and the lion shall eat straw like the ox.
The nursing child shall play over the hole of the asp,
   and the weaned child shall put its hand on the adder's den.
They will not hurt or destroy
   on all [God's] holy mountain,

for the earth will be full of the knowledge of the Lord
as the waters cover the sea.

In the Gospels, Jesus promises that the last will be first. Those who mourn will laugh. The meek will inherit the earth. The oppressed will occupy seats of honor. The poor will feast on the finest of foods. The incarcerated will go free. The sick will be healed. The dead will rise.

This is the language of reversal. Of justice that restores and renews all people and all things. This is the language of sin, in all its guises, being unmade. These are words of salvation, in all its possibilities, being fully realized.

I understand why we hesitate. All of this sounds far too good to be true. But it's not. It's not, because God is not. If God insists on creation-wide healing and justice, then God is capable of more than we have yet seen, imagined, or hoped for. It's the human impossibility of God's far-reaching vision that makes it credible and trustworthy: what is utterly out of our reach is more than possible for God.

There are still days when I grieve for the little girl I used to be. The little girl who spent so much time on her knees, chasing an elusive salvation. How many years did she spend on that cramped stage, acting out her hopeless drama with God?

If I could, I'd gather her into my arms and tell her what I believe now. Salvation is so much roomier than she knows. God's favorite human emotion isn't shame. The concrete wall she's pressing against is not of God's making, and the hands she's skinning bare against it are already covered in her Savior's. She can turn away from the wall now. A God who loves her is waiting.

7 | CONSENTING TO BROKENNESS: LAMENT

"We are Easter people!" That's a line I heard often as a little girl, and one I took very much to heart. Easter was my favorite church holiday, even more so than Christmas. I loved waking up before dawn on those chilly New England mornings each April, putting on a flowery pink dress, and driving down to the pier with my parents for our Easter sunrise service. I loved our church's main services even more: the trumpets that accompanied the choir's opening procession, the impassioned preaching, the pews stuffed with people in dapper clothes and pastel hats, and the glorious "Hallelujah Chorus" that finished off the morning. Most of all, I loved the moment in the service when my father stood up and shouted, "He is risen!" and all of us shouted back, "He is risen indeed!"

But being Easter, people extended far beyond the festivities of Holy Week. I understood that as God's children, we were the recipients, and hence the bearers, of good news—the best good news to ever hit the planet. This meant we had a responsibility to present a certain face to the world. A joyful face! A victorious face! Our calling was to exude joy, light, and hope to everyone around us so that they would be drawn to the good news, too. God wanted people of celebration—people filled with the peace that passes all understanding.

Consequently, the sacred stories I inherited as a child were happily-ever-after stories with very particular plotlines. There was the deliverance plot, the healing plot, the uplift plot, and the faded-scars-are-okay-but-open-wounds-are-*not* plot. The dialogue included statements like: "My doctor says the cancer is too advanced to treat, but God is a God of miracles. By his stripes we are healed!" "My daughter has been a prodigal for years, but God is faithful. My little girl will come back to the faith!" "I never thought I'd lose my husband this young, but God wanted him in heaven and I trust God's plan."

I heard and read these kinds of testimonies all the time, and to this day I believe they were earnest, faithful, and well intentioned. But something about them rang hollow, too. They sounded like redacted legal documents; I could see key lines blocked out in black Sharpie on each page. Grief barely showed up in these documents at all, and when it did, it was couched in platitude or apology. Sorrow was dirty laundry, and a guilty embarrassment filled the room if anyone aired it. After all, what would happen if unbelievers saw *unhappy* Christians? What would happen to our witness?

To be fair, the good people with whom I grew up and the many Christians who still espouse this brand of forced positivity come by it honestly. We live in a grief-phobic and efficiency-obsessed culture that encourages us to approach sorrow as labor. As burden. As task. This is clear even in the verbs we typically associate with grief: We work through grief. We manage grief. We process grief, and we handle, bear, endure, survive, and overcome it. I never hear anyone say, "I welcome grief." Or "I honor grief." Or even "I'm making time for grief."

So it didn't occur to me for a long time that faithful people can grieve as an act of faith. I didn't know that sorrow isn't something to hide, manage, or process in the Christian tradition but rather that it's something to honor as a sacred practice. In the biblical tradition, sorrow is no less faithful or truthful than joy. It is a treasure to receive with open, trusting hands. It's a loving gift offered by a generous God, to help us become more authentic human beings in a broken world.

———————

I practiced a grief-averse faith for a long time, well into adulthood. I practiced it even after its narrowness began to close in on me, making my spiritual life small, flat, and shallow. I slapped a neat theological bow on circumstances that called for nuance and complexity: "Everything happens for a reason." "God doesn't give us more than we can bear." "'Rejoice' is a command." I felt my own inauthenticity every time I said these things, but I had no other language for the brokenness I saw around me, so I said them anyway.

I had read the famous line of St. Irenaeus, and I knew that "the glory of God is a human being fully alive." But I didn't know that "full aliveness" included emotional aliveness. A capacity to respond to life's varied experiences with depth and sensitivity. I didn't know that full aliveness requires us to sit honestly with the whole spectrum of human experience—joyful and sorrowful, good and bad. So I kept my "aliveness" bright, shiny, and brittle, shoving anything that hurt, angered, bewildered, or frightened me below the surface, out of sight.

And then? Life happened, as it inevitably will. I left home, finished college and graduate school, got married, and became a mother. And within a few short years of bringing our precious

daughter into the world, my husband and I found ourselves learning a very new vocabulary of faith and doubt. The language of
desperation. Bewilderment. Grief and deep fear.

We watched, stunned and largely helpless, as our daughter's
beautiful sensitivity and responsiveness to the world morphed
into anxiety, obsessive-compulsive disorder, depression, anorexia,
and self-harm. It was as if all the lights in the house of faith went
out, leaving us in deep shadow as we tried and tried to hold our
baby back from the abyss.

A few years after these life-threatening struggles for our
daughter began, our fourteen-year-old son had a bike accident
on his way home from school. He remembers waking up on the
asphalt with a cracked helmet, a few scrapes, and what turned
out to be a vicious post-concussive headache. At the time of this
writing, it has been five years since the accident. Five years of lost
schooling, failed medical treatments, and deep loneliness. And
still the headache persists.

When my daughter first started battling mental illness, and
again during the first weeks and months after my son's accident,
I received many varieties of advice, "encouragement," and reassurance. All of it was couched in the language of a grief-free,
pain-free Christianity. "God is doing this to deepen your prayer
life—just have faith," people told me. "God has a plan, and it's
only ever for your good." "Your children are being prepared for
something amazing." "This is going to end in a miraculous healing, we know it—that's God's promise."

What I wanted but didn't receive was an invitation to scream.
To cry. To throw things. To pound my fists at God, ask why, and
fall apart. I realized then, in fits and starts, that the faith I'd cultivated since childhood was much too small for the reality my

family was facing. If God really wanted me to smile and sing praise songs as my daughter starved herself and my son lived in a darkened bedroom to manage his pain, I could no longer remain a Christian.

Long story short: the experience of mothering two children who are not okay has demolished any lingering, inherited platitudes about faith, blessing, healing, immunity, and joy. As I've watched both children suffer in ways I didn't even know were possible before I became a parent, I've had to unlearn most of what I thought I knew about God, joy, faith, and victory.

I've discovered that loss, sorrow, doubt, and finitude are not bizarre exceptions in the life of faith. Often, they are the water we drink and the air we breathe in a broken, yearning world that is not yet what God would have it be. I've learned to accept that shredded hope—hope drenched in tears, hope articulated in full-bodied groans and wails and screams—still counts as hope.

At the same time, I've embraced a roomier and far more generous understanding of God's nearness. Sometimes God is present not *despite* our grievous circumstances but *in* them. Not in flashy, spectacular ways, but in the small, mundane graces that make life bearable in the storm. Brief moments that are pain-free. Twenty-four hours without an anxiety attack. An unexpected burst of laughter after an absurd doctor's appointment. The kindness of friends and strangers. The weekly rhythms of liturgy and the Eucharist. The subtle shift in perspective that comes every time I stop trying to flee from grief and decide instead that "here"—this place, this time, this circumstance, this sorrow—is holy.

Bearing witness as my loved ones suffer—not briefly, but over long stretches of time—has taught me to recognize God's presence in all things, even in God's apparent absence. Even in the hunger that causes me to yearn, ask, seek, and knock. Even in the bitterness of my own disappointments. A roomy Christianity insists that God is as fully present in my lament as in my happiness.

Learning to make room for grief as a sacred gift has literally saved my faith. It has kept me from withdrawing into a small, hollow, and embittered life. It has kept my heart from hardening. It has brought me back from treacherous descents into resentment, cynicism, and jealousy. And it has taught me to notice and celebrate even the tiniest eruptions of grace and joy.

So why do Christians avoid grief so avidly? And how might we learn to stop? There are many reasons, but here are some that resonate powerfully for me.

First, we mistake grief for faithlessness. This is the belief I internalized as a child. The harmful belief that if we're good Christians, we shouldn't entertain doubts, fears, sorrows, or complaints in our relationship with God, because to do so is to flunk the test of faith.

To the contrary, I've learned that grief—or to use its biblical synonym, *lament*—is an act of the boldest faith. When we dare to lament openly, we're recognizing that what *is* is not yet what it should be. We're insisting that we were created for more, called to more, and destined for more. When we grieve, something deep within us names the terrible disconnect between God's dream for a healed and restored world and the brokenness that's still pervasive all around us.

Our grief bears witness to a gospel that is hardy enough and resilient enough to face the world as it is and still declare the coming of God's kingdom. We don't need to sugarcoat reality to make the story of Jesus true and compelling. God is not fragile. The gospel isn't breakable. A faith that's founded on a cross, a broken body, and a wounded Savior can withstand whatever the world throws at it. When we grieve, we name these things as true. We insist on them, and that insistence itself is an act of faith.

On the other hand, the human cost of tiptoeing around God's supposed frailty is staggering. I've watched many people I love do this, and I've done it myself. We'll dare for just an instant to name an honest experience: "I'm furious at God right now," or "My faith is doing nothing for me in the midst of this pain." Then immediately we'll back away as if lightning might strike: "But it's okay! I have so much to be grateful for. I need to focus on the future. All shall be well."

What's at stake here is not whether such faith claims are true. What's at stake is authenticity, both ours and God's. If the God we've staked our lives on is too delicate to bear the hard truth of our lives, then why have we bothered with the gospel in the first place?

Sometimes we need to forgive God. I know that many Christians find this idea disrespectful, because it doesn't jibe with the official equation: humans offend, God forgives. But reality is more complicated. As Christians, we live in the gap between God's absolute goodness and the world's catastrophic brokenness. There's no way to live truthfully in this gap without naming the fact that sometimes God lets us down. God lets us down by God's inaction. By God's silence. By God's hiddenness. These aren't moral failures on God's part. But they nonetheless grieve, disappoint, and anger us.

When I read the Bible, I'm struck by the radical honesty of the characters we consider saints. They weren't afraid to express their disappointment in God and to acknowledge that sometimes they may even need to forgive God.

"O my God, I cry by day, but you do not answer; and by night, but find no rest," David cries out in the Psalms (22:2). "He has torn me in his wrath, and hated me," says Job (16:9). "[I'm] angry enough to die," mutters Jonah (4:9). "My eyes are spent with weeping; my stomach churns; my bile is poured out on the ground because of the destruction of my people," says the writer of Lamentations (2:11). "My God, my God, why have you forsaken me?" Jesus himself groans on the cross (Matthew 27:46).

If I'm reading correctly, these people aren't accusing God of sinfulness. They're naming God's failure to meet their fiercest and most tender hopes and expectations. They're calling out the unfairness of a world in which terrible things happen to frail and helpless people. They're articulating the scandal of a disappointing God.

But God? God is not scandalized in response. God honors the fact that these spiritual ancestors of ours cling to God even when it hurts them to do so. God listens, even when the only prayers the people can make with integrity are prayers of outrage.

Struggling to forgive God might be our best protection against spiritual apathy or despair. Forgiving God keeps God vibrant and relevant in our lives—not as a dusty relic but as a force to reckon with.

So we sometimes mistake grief for faithlessness. Second, we fear that grief might compromise our witness. As believers in

Jesus, we worry that our sorrows, if articulated honestly, might cast a shadow on Christianity, making it harder for people curious about the faith to walk through our doors.

I'm convinced now that the opposite is true. Pews are emptying not because we practice robust lament on Sunday mornings but because we don't. I think that churches in America are struggling because we've lost our fluency in the language of lament. It's consequential that Christians don't have a good track record when it comes to balancing a commitment to joy with a sensitive and holistic response to the world's pain. Too often we are known for exhibiting, and demanding, a Pollyanna-ish cheerfulness that refuses to look the complexities of life in the face. We behave as if our faith—and, by extension, our God—is too fragile to handle life's harsh side without a generous side dish of grinning emojis.

Christianity, if it's going to be credible and life giving, cannot be about denialism, or shallow sentiment, or cheap grace. As followers of Jesus, we're not called to be happy-clappy worshippers who keep ourselves at a remove from pain—our own or anyone else's. We're called to live, speak, and serve from deep, authentic places. In this sense, grief is a powerful witness to the ongoing relevance of the gospel. It gives us credibility.

"I am most disillusioned with the Christian faith when in the presence of a Christian who refuses to name the traumas of this world," writes activist and liturgist Cole Arthur Riley. "I am suspicious of anyone who can observe colonization, genocide, and decay in the world and not be stirred to lament in some way. When I watch somebody name what should not be and earnestly question God about it, I immediately become a fraction of the skeptic I am. Lament is a very compelling apologetic."

Third, we Americans tend to practice an "island" spirituality, one more individualistic than communal. Our Lone Ranger culture does not encourage us to live with a deep sense of our connectedness to all of creation. This makes grief of a biblical variety very difficult, because the practice of lament we see in Scripture is very communal. It expresses the pain of a whole people. It protests entire systems of oppression and exploitation. It names sins that go far beyond the insular and individual. Lament is a big, shared grief that spills out everywhere.

Lament insists that, in fact, we are not islands; we are deeply connected, one to the other. The pain of one is the pain of all. Our peace isn't peace, our justice isn't justice, our safety isn't safety, and our wholeness isn't wholeness if we secure them only for ourselves and those in our immediate circles. Grief calls us to implicate ourselves in stories larger than our own, less comfortable than our own, less familiar than our own. It asks us to take responsibility for a collective that encompasses all races, genders, cultures, sexualities, and economic situations. Lament makes it impossible for us to isolate ourselves within our own cocoons of blessing. It resists the American myth of self-sufficiency and pulls us deep into the whole fabric of God's creation.

The fourth reason we avoid lament is because we want to forget, and grief requires remembrance. In his powerful book on grief, *The Wild Edge of Sorrow*, Jungian analyst Francis Weller writes that "the two primary sins of Western civilization are amnesia and anesthesia: we forget and we go numb." Grief asks us to refrain from both. It asks us to revisit the unhealed wounds of our pasts, both personal and collective, and allow those wounds to move and motivate us. It asks us to dwell in the stories and traumas of our ancestors: the people we've lost, the people we've harmed, the people we've ignored, the people we've rendered invisible to secure our own comforts. Whether we're talking about the millions we've lost to the Covid-19 pandemic, the traumas of our own childhoods, the family secrets that haunt our nights, the horrors inflicted on the Indigenous communities of this continent, the legacy of slavery in the United States, or the countless species we've lost to human-induced climate change, grief asks us to remember. To linger. To honor with our concerted attention. This is hard to do in a culture that encourages us to forget and move on as quickly as possible. Why disrupt the status quo with inconvenient memories?

Grief is subversive in part because it fundamentally changes our relationship to the past, the present, and the future. It messes with our complacency, asking us to disrupt and evolve. We can't do these things if we're invested in forgetting what lies behind us. We can't do these things if we're busy gripping the present with frantic hands, struggling to keep everything the same as it is right now.

And the fifth reason we turn away from lament: We like to stay in our heads. But grief requires embodiment. It requires us to integrate soul and body. I'll confess that this reason definitely applies to me. I tend to practice my faith from the head up. I like ideas and abstractions, because I can control them far more easily than I can my tears. At some deep level, I worry that if I really give in to grief—give in to the messy, gritty, noisy, sloppy expressions of my sorrows—I won't find my way back out. I worry that I'll come across as undignified. Out of control. Blurry at the edges.

To state the obvious, grief requires us to feel. To mourn, to hurt, to ache. To relinquish control and trust that what lies on the other side of full-bodied lament is something beautiful and worthwhile. Grief is an incarnate gift, one we have to receive with our hands and feet, our hearts and guts. It's easier to turn away from suffering when we abstract it and hold ourselves apart from it. It's much harder to turn away when we allow the suffering to penetrate our skin and rattle our bones. Lament is hard: it costs us, emotionally, so we avoid it.

But we will never heal ourselves or this world if we choose a safe, pious detachment from pain and suffering. At some point, our failure to grieve will harden and calcify our hearts. It will make us brisk, efficient, tidy, and cold. It will put us at a fatal remove from the Jesus who wept over his beloved Jerusalem, cried at his friend Lazarus's grave, and wailed from the cross in despair at his Father's silence. At the risk of being too blunt: if we won't grieve, we won't love.

———

The first time someone told me that the practice of lament is biblical, I didn't believe her. At the time, I hadn't yet learned how to read Scripture with my senses and my imagination. I didn't know how to engage the Bible through the clarifying lens of grief. Since then, I've learned that truly powerful things can happen when I come to God's Word as I am, in my sorrow. When I look for the ways in which a Gospel story, a psalm, an epistle, or a prophetic poem might make room for grief, lament becomes a gift I can unwrap and fold into my life.

I stumbled into this way of reading a few years ago, when I was preparing to preach a sermon. The Scripture text was a very familiar one, from the Gospel of Mark. A woman who's been bleeding for twelve years dares to approach Jesus and secretly touch his cloak. Her bleeding immediately stops. But before she can disappear back into the crowd, Jesus, noticing that power has gone out from his body, stops, turns, and insists on finding out who touched him.

I had read the story countless times before and thought I knew it inside out. But seemingly out of nowhere, one line from the story suddenly blew the story wide open: "But the woman, knowing what had happened to her, came in fear and trembling, fell down before him, and told him the whole truth" (Mark 5:33).

The only way I know how to describe what happened next is that time stopped—as in, *narrative* time stopped. In my imagination, that moment—when the woman knelt, opened her trembling mouth, and allowed all the words that had been dammed up inside of her body for so many years to come pouring out— stretched and stretched and stretched, into a kind of eternity. In my imagination, minutes passed. Hours passed. Days passed. The sun set and the stars came out, rain fell and wind blew and dawn broke, and still: still, Jesus listened and the woman spoke.

Why? Because it was the whole truth. That's what Mark says: she told him the *whole* truth. And when you've been shattered as that woman had been shattered, when you've had your most desperate hope disappointed more times than you can count, when all the institutions—cultural, medical, and religious—that were supposed to help you have so epically failed, when no one has touched you for over a decade because the porousness of your body has rendered you unworthy of their tenderness: how long would it take you to tell that whole truth? I imagine it took a long, long time. And still—*still*—Jesus held space for her. He created a sacred container into which she could pour her story. He

117

honored her need to speak about her grief. The truth of it. The ache of it. The grief of it. The whole truth.

If Jesus invited us to tell him the whole truth right now, I wonder what stories we would tell. Would it be a story about the Covid-19 pandemic? Would it be a story about doubt? About not knowing how to reconcile the good news of the gospel with the questions we have, with the sorrows we carry, with a planet tipping hard and fast toward climate catastrophe? Would it be a story about our bodies—how they're changing, aging, or failing? Would it be the childhood stories we've carried for a long time, hoping they'll fade away because we're not sure we'll survive the telling? Would it be a story about something happening in our country or in the world? Wars and rumors of wars? The scourge of gun violence? The long shadows of systemic racism?

If Jesus's tender encounter with the woman in Mark's Gospel represents the rule and not the exception, then we have permission to tell the whole truth. The heart of God is big enough to hold it.

In his collection of micro-essays, *The Book of Delights*, Ross Gay writes about our culture's urgent need for communal lament—for holy spaces where our sorrows can mingle and join:

> It astonishes me sometimes—no, often—how every person I get to know—everyone, regardless of everything, by which I mean everything—lives with some profound personal sorrow. Brother addicted. Mother murdered. Dad died in surgery. Rejected by their family. Cancer came back. Evicted. Fetus not okay. Everyone, regardless, always, of everything. Not to mention the existential

sorrow we all might be afflicted with, which is that we, and what we love, will soon be annihilated. Which sounds more dramatic than it might. Let me just say dead. Is this sorrow the great wilderness? Is sorrow the true wild? And if it is—and if we join them—your wild to mine—what's that? For joining, too, is a kind of annihilation. What if we joined our sorrows, I'm saying. I'm saying: What if that is joy?

I still believe that we're Easter people. But even the Easter stories we cherish in the Gospels make room for ache, fear, regret, and sorrow. In Mark's version—the version we tend not to read so often in church—we get no glimpses of the risen Jesus on Easter morning. Peter and the other disciples are nowhere to be seen. When a young man in a white robe tells Mary Magdalene and her two companions that Jesus has been raised from the dead, the women don't cry out in joy; they respond with "alarm," "terror," and "amazement." The angel's announcement of good news inspires neither belief nor transformation. We witness no Easter proclamation, no narrative arc from hopelessness to certitude. Instead, we witness fear, flight, and silence (Mark 16:5–8).

I am so grateful that our ancestors in the faith decided to keep Mark's version in our canon. Because we need it. Sometimes, just like the women on that first Easter morning, we need time. We might hear what the angel at the tomb is saying to us, and in some deep recess of our souls we might recognize that the angel's words—"He has been raised; he is not here"—are the most consequential words we'll ever hear. But we're still trembling in alarm. We're still trying not to flee.

And that's okay.

It's okay to sit with the terror and the amazement that must fall upon us when God's incomprehensible work of redemption collides in real time with the broken bewilderment of our lives. Mark's slow Easter assures us that we don't need to shout right away. Sometimes it's okay to fall silent first. To run. To wait. To whisper.

Sometimes, when human beings are in profound pain, good news hurts. We find it too jarring, too dissonant, too grating. We can't map it, we can't bridge it, we can't wrap language around it. We literally can't take it into our bodies; something tender and essential within us resists. At such moments, maybe the most faithful response to the seeming disconnect between Christ's resurrection and our continuing pain is honesty. The honesty of silence. Of tears. Of fear. Of grief. The women at the tomb waited before they spoke; they led with wounded awe, not premature consolation.

We often shy away from Mark's version of Easter because we don't trust the story itself to do its work; we feel some pious need to protect and embellish it. (Even later editors of Mark's Gospel felt the need to smooth out its jagged conclusion with a rounder, happier ending.) But if the resurrection really is the best good news that has ever hit the planet, then its goodness doesn't depend on us. It doesn't matter one bit if we believe on the spot or not. The tomb is empty. Death is vanquished. Jesus lives. Period. We are not in charge of Easter; God is.

In fact, Jesus's own resurrected body speaks to the importance of lament in the midst of joy. Even in the most triumphant story ever told in Scripture or history, scars remain (John 20:27). The embodied memory of pain, loss, trauma, and suffering remains. Yes, God works life out of death. Yes, God redeems and restores. But Jesus's resurrection is not an erasure of his past. Restoration is not a "making okay" via the promise of new prosperity. Resurrection is a way forward from the grave that honors the scars we carry, helping us to bear them with resilience and hope.

We become fully alive when we realize that the gospel is astonishingly supple. It holds joy and grief together not in contrast but in conversation, and in relationship, and in some sort of honest becoming. Better still, this messy, roomy place is precisely where God loves to show up. God dwells in the roomy place where pain and possibility, delight and despair, muck and miracle crash into each other.

8 | BEARING GOD'S IMAGE: WOMEN

It's early on a January morning, the sky still dark, and my mother is heating a saucepan of milk on the stove. She's wearing a sari, as usual, and its neatly pleated *palloo* hangs invitingly over her shoulder. I sneak up behind her in my fuzzy pink pajamas, grab a fistful of the soft fabric, and spin. Caught entirely by surprise, she turns in circles, struggling to catch me. She barely avoids a burn as she tugs at the tangled sari in my fingers, but I laugh, spinning until I'm dizzy. When I finally let go, she reorganizes herself like a ruffled hen, pinches my ear in mock punishment, and presses me against her stomach. I'm dizzy and four years old, in perpetual orbit around her.

Growing up, I don't call her "Mommy" unless white people are listening. Like all the children in my Anglicized Indian family, I say "Mummy." Sometimes "Ma," or "Mumma," or "Umma," the proper Malayalam word for mother. But who she is, truly, is *Mummy*. Not like the Egyptian dead. Not like snooty British films. More like when you eat something good and close your mouth fast to keep the taste in longer.

Barely five feet tall, Mummy nevertheless reigns in our second-floor apartment, a blur of efficient, Proverbs 31 womanhood. She cooks, bakes, gardens, and crochets. Teaches Sunday school, sells Avon, prepares huge feasts for my father's church events, teaches me how to read and write, and works night shifts at a camera company to help pay the bills. Her warm skin smells like sandalwood, bleach, fresh earth, and spices. She is my world. Its center is her warm, soft body, its outer rim the close, tight path I spin.

Until my parents buy a house in the suburbs, which happens when I'm twelve, we live on the second floor of an eight-unit apartment building in Cambridge, Massachusetts. It's a building filled with immigrants and their second-generation children: Greeks, Cambodians, Laotians, Indians. When I'm six, my parents buy the building, and soon five of the eight apartments house Indian families, many of them our relatives. Saris and salwars hang on the laundry lines. The hallways smell like curry, and aunties with soft hands fuss over my hair.

Against this backdrop—tailing, adoring, and fearing my mother—I become a Good Christian Girl. This becoming is not a given in my childhood world; it's a high-stakes apprenticeship, riddled with obstacles and dangers. The possibility of becoming Something Else—something wild, unfeminine, scandalous, and bad—looms ever and large, so my mother directs my formative quest at all times. She takes my limbs and teaches me how to manage them. Hands in lap, feet on floor, knees together. She explains the proper order of things in God's good world—the hierarchies of male and female, leader and follower, headship and submission. With words and without them, she teaches me that a godly woman's glory is in effacement, in quietness, in not putting herself crassly forward.

At the dinner table, my mother serves first and eats last. On sidewalks, no matter how slowly my father walks, my mother lags a few respectful yards behind him. In church, she is a model of feminine propriety, her headscarf pulled over her black curls, her sari draped close, her eyes cast modestly downward.

I do my best to imitate her, because she exudes the beauty, piety, and dignity I want for myself. As a little girl, I want to be just like her. I want to please God just as she does.

But all the while, I worry. I worry because my imitation isn't wholehearted. I worry because God's "good order" doesn't feel good; it feels cruel and unfair. I worry because, while I've been told that I bear God's image, I wonder: How can I, when I'm never allowed to stand tall?

———————

I am twenty-two, and it's the day before my Big Fat Indian Wedding. The women in my extended family have traveled from far and wide to gather in my mother's kitchen to cook, clean, laugh, and tell stories. For hours they sit cross-legged on the tile floor, peeling onions, grating ginger, crushing cardamom. "Just sit with us and rest," they say each time I offer to help, and I do. This is my night to have my cheeks pinched and my fingers caressed in strong, calloused hands. It is my night to listen and learn, in this intimate, women-only version of premarital counseling. My mother, grandmother, aunts, and cousins have lessons to teach.

As the hours pass, the stories of these women's lives and experiences flow. Some are warm and pleasant: the engagements, the pregnancies, the births, the graduations. But others are not. I learn about the blustery, loudmouthed uncle who bawls like a baby if he gets so much as a paper cut. About the son-in-law who talks big at church but doesn't even know how to boil water for tea without burning his hands. About the preacher-grandpa who fires off ferocious sermons on Sunday mornings but can't find matching socks without his wife's help. About a young cousin who tenderly calls his new bride "brilliant" at home but would sooner die than confess such admiration in public.

The women never say the unspeakable thing out loud, but their stories communicate a two-part secret, a secret they're convinced will save me as I embark on the twin adventures of womanhood and marriage. Part One: Men are officially in charge because that's what God—also male, after all—wants them to be. There's nothing we can do about this, since God is all-knowing and wise and we trust his ordering of things. Part Two: We must still run things behind the scenes—carefully, without drawing attention to ourselves—because, in fact, men are incompetent babies.

The humorous and poignant gap between these two gender narratives—the official story and the unofficial one—is never named. But by the time those mountains of onions are peeled and chopped the night before my wedding, I understand a few things very well. I understand that women have tremendous savvy about the worlds they occupy, and that I am blessed to be surrounded by their fierce and unshakable love.

And I understand that the life's work of these good, smart, courageous women is to live with poise and dignity in the very gap that holds them back: to dandle men, fuss over them, indulge them, and forgive them, all the while cherishing their own secret superiority. Our strength and solace will never lie in institutions; the institutions belong to men, as God has ordained. But we women have a secret—a powerful secret we acknowledge only with smiles, winks, and occasional wisecracks. This secret is the best we've got; it salvages our dignity, helps us survive, and somehow gives us the last laugh.

I go to bed that night before my wedding with a deep ache in my heart. I'm grateful that I get to be among such remarkable older women. But I want more. More for them. More for the men they feel they have to "manage." More for myself.

———————

In *Wearing God: Clothing, Laughter, Fire, and Other Overlooked Ways of Meeting God*, writer and Episcopal priest Lauren Winner describes how the images, titles, pronouns, and other descriptors we use for God affect us psychologically, culturally, and spiritually. She writes that the characteristics (visual, physical, metaphorical) we attribute to God always reflect and reinforce the characteristics we value most highly in society. The *body* we give to God always reflects and reinforces the hierarchies we impose on human bodies. As feminist theologian Mary Daly puts it so forcefully, "If God is male then male is God."

I grew up with an exclusively male and masculine God. While the adults in my life would have insisted that God is technically beyond sex and gender—a divine Spirit without genitalia, transcending all human descriptors—such workarounds had zero impact on me as a child and young woman, because they ignored the tremendous power of language to construct, instill, and consolidate reality. The official teaching of a non-sexed, non-gendered God completely dismissed the formative influence of sermons, Bible stories, and hymns in which God was always and only "he." "He" the warrior, the father, the husband, the king. The effect wasn't simply intellectual. The God I took into my bones and enthroned in my subconscious self was male.

Though I read and studied my Bible faithfully, I didn't learn that *ruach*—the God-Spirit who hovers over the unformed earth in Genesis 1:2—is feminine. I didn't discover Sophia, the feminine spirit of wisdom (Proverbs 8:22) who companions God in the work of creation. No one told me about God the pregnant woman moaning in childbirth (Isaiah 42:14), or God the ferocious she-bear (Hosea 13:8), or God the soaring mother eagle (Deuteronomy 32:11–12). I had no idea that God is a compassionate and competent midwife (Psalm 22:9–10), or that Jesus describes himself as a yearning mother hen (Matthew 23:37; Luke 13:34).

In a broader sense, I didn't know that the Bible's overabundance of images for the Divine—rock, bread, gate, shepherd, tree, vine, water, flame—might serve to warn us *away* from emphasizing one over the others. That the Bible's generosity in this regard was meant to safeguard us from literalism, patriarchal or otherwise.

But I know that if I'd noticed the diversity of biblical representations and asked about them when I was growing up, someone in charge would have explained that what really matters *is* the literal, not the figurative. Not the "mere" metaphors. As in, "Sure, it's possible that God is *like* a mother or a midwife or a she-bear or a hen. But God *is* Father." They would have also reminded me that Jesus addressed God as Father. Proof, in their minds, that no other address is permissible.

Yet the incredibly intelligent and gifted women I grew up around had a lot to say about the work of God in their non-male lives. They're the ones who taught me how to pray, how to listen, how to worship, how to love. But in the Christian world that raised me, their spiritual gifts were not the ones that really counted. This was true in our homes, but it was even truer in the churches that first formed me as a Christian. The very same women who skillfully juggled careers, marriage, motherhood, friendship, spiritual practice, and all manner of recreational pursuits when they were outside our church walls deferred to men completely when they walked inside. No one asked if this dynamic was life-giving. No one wondered aloud if it gave men and women a well-rounded experience of God, or strengthened the church, or bolstered our witness, or reflected the full liberatory message of Scripture and the gospel.

I had to leave the faith communities of my childhood to learn that the first person to name God in Scripture is Hagar, a trafficked woman who births a nation. Or that the first abolitionists and justice warriors who stand up to Pharaoh in the book of Exodus are not Moses and Aaron but Shiphrah and Puah, two midwives. Or that women in the Hebrew Bible serve as mothers, yes, but also as prophets, judges, warriors, and counselors.

Years before Jesus says, "This is my body, given for you," a young teenager named Mary says it by offering her whole self—mind, heart, will, intellect, hands, feet, uterus, birth canal—in bold service to God. The first missionary named in the Gospels is a Samaritan woman who questions her way to a robust faith in Jesus—and then, by the power of her preaching, brings her entire city into the fold of the gospel. The minister who pours oil over Jesus's head and anoints him into kingship is his friend Mary, the sister of Martha and Lazarus. The first witness to the resurrection—the apostle to the apostles—is Mary Magdalene.

My intention in contrasting stories from my upbringing with those in Scripture is not to devalue the forms of power that exist and thrive below the surface, in the margins, and off the record. These forms are formidable, creative, and very often beautiful.

The women in Scripture exercise them, too, and God blesses their efforts. I will always be grateful for the examples of quiet, "secret" leadership and authority I saw growing up.

But I also know how disempowering it was to be female in a religious tradition that didn't *see* me as fully and generously as it saw my male counterparts. I know how small and suffocating Christianity can still feel for girls and women in many corners of the contemporary church. They are no less the image-bearers of God than boys and men, but their communities of faith won't allow them to live deeply and boldly into the divine likeness which is their birthright.

Oddly, the God they're taught to worship doesn't mind if they use the full range of their gifts and talents in the secular world. They can run companies, perform surgery, teach in universities, sit on the Supreme Court, and govern nations. But in the church, this same God supposedly desires their respectful silence. I know first-hand how bewildering this kind of forced compartmentalization— this splitting of "secular life" from "sacred life"—can be. It makes impossible the holistic, integrated lives the gospel invites all of us to live.

But the problem is not *just* that a narrow conception of God locks women out of the halls of ecclesiastical power. It's also that such narrowness keeps us from seeing the correlation between God as male and the church's historic reluctance to acknowledge, expose, and compassionately address the horrors of sexual abuse. Between the church's male centeredness and its lack of a collective will to stamp out domestic violence, sexual harassment, toxic masculinity, and rape culture. Between the sexist language that flows from the pulpit and the deep shame so many girls and women internalize around their bodies.

I no longer attend a church that reserves the priesthood for men, or discourages women from exercising their spiritual gifts, or insists on male-only descriptions for God. This is a tremendous gift, and I don't take it for granted. Yet I worry that we who attend egalitarian churches might assume the work is finished and forget that for many women, questions of justice, inclusion, empowerment, and belonging burn on.

A roomy church—a church that embraces the "many rooms" of a spacious and hospitable Christianity—will give people of all genders and sexual orientations the space they need to name, to lament, to rage, and to integrate what has been lost and can't be recovered. I can't get my childhood back. I can't unmake the male God the church formed in me before I had the tools to comprehend what was happening.

On my own, I could never have found my way to a God who is bigger, richer, deeper, and wider than the male deity I inherited. The church has to take the lead in this work, endorsing language and imagery that is far more comprehensive than the language we've been given. We need the church to walk with us as we learn to articulate our faith in this new tongue.

In her book *A Big-Enough God: A Feminist's Search for a Joyful Theology*, Sara Maitland explains why she uses female pronouns for God while at the same time retaining the language of God's fatherhood. That joining, she argues, is essential for a truly emancipatory theology:

> In God, in her Fatherhood, the fathers of this world are to be set at naught, stripped of their privileges and made into servants. They think they are mighty, but they will be put down from their seats by the God who is almighty,

and the poor and the hungry, the humbled and the meek will be exalted.

For God's is no fatherhood as we have learned it from our fathers; it is not a fatherhood of power, but of equality. It is not a fatherhood of authority, but of unity. It is not a fatherhood of domination, of rape and abuse and sexism, but a fatherhood of love. . . .

She is Father in relation to the patriarchy; she is Father so that the power of the Fathers will be broken. She is Father in relation to the Trinity so that fathers can be given a model of how they ought to be. She is Father so that the little ones of the earth—the oppressed, the poor, the widows and orphans—may be set free from patriarchy and sing their triumph.

While I'm increasingly drawn to God as Mother, I also love Maitland's generous revisioning of God's (feminine) Fatherhood. I love its potent critique of abusive, male-centered power. I love it for the room it gives each one of us, in all of our gender diversity, to find in God the freedom to live fully into the *imago Dei*. To surrender power and embrace vulnerability. To learn the hard lessons of humility. To make self-giving love our beginning and our end. If "she is Father," then no one is outside of her purview. No one is beyond the reach of this God and her fatherly capacity to save, equalize, liberate, and bless.

There are many ways to make the case for a more expansive Christianity for women, and I've alluded to several already: The abundance of feminine imagery for God in Scripture. The essential and authoritative roles women play in both the Hebrew Bible and the New Testament. The political, cultural, psychological, and spiritual dangers that lie in *not* embracing a roomy feminism in the church.

But for me, the heart of the matter lies with Jesus himself—or, more specifically, with the incarnation. God decided to embrace a fully embodied humanity, to take on flesh and live among us. This might sound odd, because I've often heard people make the opposite argument: "But Jesus was a *man*. He came to earth *as a man*. Doesn't that tell you something important about God's design for male headship and authority?"

It doesn't, and here's why: The true shock and scandal of the incarnation lies in its particularity. Jesus doesn't come to earth as a generic, ahistorical, nonspecific human. He doesn't take on an abstract and idealized flesh in order to save us. He takes on the *particular* flesh of a first-century itinerant Jewish peasant: poor, colonized, and criminalized. It is out of his radical specificity that Jesus includes, embraces, and saves us, in all our specificity.

Philosopher Michael Fitzpatrick articulates it this way:

The Gospel is only good news because Jesus comes as a slave, a powerless peasant in occupied Judea. It's because he comes in this particular human life that an untouchable in India, a Syrian refugee, a young teenager with Tourette's, and a black woman living under apartheid can each know that regardless of what the powerful in their society decree, the Creator has unconditionally acted to liberate *them*. Far from being ashamed of their bodies, God took their bodies, their flesh, their very skin and infirmities as [God's] own. Wherever human flesh is declared repugnant to God, *that* is the flesh in which the Word comes. . . .

Only if Jesus' embodiment of God includes my flesh can I find saving hope. Thankfully I am assured that Christ died for me because Christ took particular Jewish flesh. That Jesus was a branch from the root of Jesse testifies that Jesus is the black Christ, the female Christ, the sexually trafficked Christ, the bullied Christ, the unemployed Christ, the bulimic Christ, the Alzheimer's Christ, and every other flesh that suffers.

As the mother of a daughter who has struggled for years to recognize the inherent beauty and dignity of her female body, I would add to Fitzpatrick's list the anorexic Christ. As a mother of a son who lives with chronic pain, I would add the aching Christ. As the survivor of childhood sexual abuse, I would add the molested Christ. As a racial minority living in the United States, I would add the brown-skinned Christ. As the daughter of immigrants, I would add the displaced Christ.

All of this is to say: God's response to every form of oppression, enslavement, marginalization, and diminishment is specific, enfleshed solidarity. Full-bodied bridging, joining, and becoming. Whenever and wherever specific human bodies are deemed "less than," Jesus says, "Here. Right here. *This* is my body."

I wonder if we struggle against this astonishing specificity and its spiritual implications in part because our culture doesn't know what to do with human fleshiness. Our own, or anyone else's. In her courageous book *See Me Naked: Stories of Sexual Exile in American Christianity*, Amy Frykholm documents the many ways in which contemporary Christians live in estrangement from their own bodies. In one of her stories, she describes what happened to a visual artist named Monica when she first encountered a nude model in an art class:

> The model came out and seated herself. Monica felt a wave of repulsion. The woman serving as a model for this drawing was nothing that she had expected. She was, for one thing, fleshy. You could see pockets of cellulite on her thighs and collected fat at the tops of her arms and at her hips. Under the lights, you could see places where she had missed shaving. She was human, a human body, and that not only surprised Monica; it made her nauseous. The words that came to her mind embarrassed her: revolting, ugly, disgusting.

I recognize Monica's repulsion; it plays out in our culture all the time. It's the repulsion that makes a forty-year-old feel hideous if she doesn't look twenty. The repulsion that tells a teenager she's fat if her thighs touch. The repulsion that celebrates photoshopped Victoria's Secret models over the real curves of real women. The repulsion that fuels the multimillion-dollar diet and cosmetics industries.

A couple of years ago, I read *An Altar in the World*, Barbara Brown Taylor's book on useful modern-day spiritual practices. I cruised through the book, smiling and nodding, until I got to a chapter titled "The Practice of Wearing Skin" and read this sentence: "Whether you are sick or well, lovely or irregular, there comes a time when it is vitally important for your spiritual health to drop your clothes, look in the mirror, and say, 'Here I am. This is the body-like-no-other that my life has shaped. I live here. This is my soul's address.'"

I remember I laughed out loud. In fact, I called a couple of friends and laughed out loud with them. "She's got to be kidding, right?" I said. "Pray naked? No way."

Now I look back on that response and grieve over it. What an impoverished view of the incarnation it assumes. To pray naked is to acknowledge that this body of mine, just as it is, is not only *acceptable* to God, but is *God's*. As in: Jesus's flesh is this flesh, too. It is in *this very flesh* that I am saved, loved, held, and called.

One of my favorite New Testament stories appears in the Gospel of Mark. Jesus is taking a break from ministry, in a gentile region far from home. He doesn't want anyone to know where he is; he's worn out, perhaps, and in dire need of solitude and rest.

But his reputation follows him everywhere, and before long, an unwanted visitor appears at the door of the house where he's staying. A Syrophoenician woman—an outsider, a non-Jew, a cultural and ethnic other—needs help. She needs Jesus to cast a demon out of her suffering daughter.

Jesus's ungenerous response has appalled biblical interpreters for centuries: "Let the children be fed first, for it is not fair to take the children's food and throw it to the dogs" (Mark 7:27). Were his words born of exhaustion? Prejudice? A still-evolving comprehension of his mission? An instructive performance for his disciples?

Had I been in the Syrophoenician woman's shoes at this moment, I would have been bewildered, enraged, and heartbroken at Jesus's seeming cruelty toward me and my child. I would have flinched and fled. So I am forever grateful to this woman, this mother, this foreigner. She, my spiritual ancestor, is memorialized in Scripture for being braver, bolder, and more resilient than I could ever be: "Sir," she replies without missing a beat, "even the dogs under the table eat the children's crumbs" (v. 28).

To his credit, Jesus responds this time with humility and grace, allowing himself to be schooled in his own gospel. He allows the unnamed woman to deconstruct his prejudice and teach him that the scope of his mission is far wider, more generous, and more inclusive than he has yet realized. "Because of your teaching," he tells her in amazement, "the demon has left your daughter."

What I love about this story is that it features a woman who insists that if the good news is going to be "good" in any meaningful sense for *anyone*, it must be good for her and her daughter, too. What's the point of setting a table for a sumptuous feast if some people have to stand and watch while others get to sit and eat their fill? What's the point of a gospel that claims to topple earthly kingdoms, powers, and hierarchies if it simply baptizes those same hierarchies and reasserts them within the beloved community of the church?

"Lord, where's *my* good news?" is what the Syrophoenician woman insists on asking Jesus, with every ounce of urgency she can muster. "Where's *my daughter's* good news? How can you be the Messiah, the Son of God, the Anointed One, if your good news is so small?"

Women have been asking this question for centuries, and many churches continue to hedge in answering it. "Because of *your* teaching," Jesus tells a woman on the margins, modeling for all time a posture of humble receptivity in the face of the Holy Spirit's prodding. The kingdom of God expands *because a woman speaks.* Because a woman teaches. She insists on her place at the table, and the house of God expands to welcome her.

9 | EMBRACING THE DISSONANCE: PARADOX

C. S. Lewis once described his faith in a way that has become foundational for me: "I believe in Christianity as I believe that the Sun has risen, not only because I see it but because by it, I see everything else."

There is a wonderful spaciousness in Lewis's claim. For him, Christianity is more than a set of propositions and aesthetically pleasing metaphors. Christianity is a lens: a way of seeing, and a means of revelation. In Lewis's view, Christianity's truthfulness lies in its ability to satisfy both our imaginations and our intellects. It is trustworthy in itself, and it is trustworthy in its capacity to reveal, illuminate, and clarify everything else we look at.

In many ways, Lewis's description has helped ease my discomfort at being many things at once: American. Indian. Bicultural. Female. Christian. His "sun" has helped illuminate my disparate identities as gifts that work well together, even when their rough edges rub against each other and cause friction. I don't have to choose between them; I can hold them all, and God will hold them all with me.

It's inevitable that the through lines of our personal histories will affect what we see and value when it comes to faith. In some deep sense, I will forever be the immigrant kid who grew up on the hyphen: between dissonant worlds, trying (with varying degrees of success) to be a bridge, to move back and forth, to translate the dissonance in both directions.

For a long time, I hated the hyphen. I didn't want to be a bridge between American culture and Indian culture. I wanted to find my place in *one* world, *one* community, *one* identity that would hold all of who I am. I wanted the same to be true in my religious life. I didn't want a dissonant, hyphenated faith. I had no desire to meet Jesus on the bridge of my own spiritual confusion.

But as I've meditated on Lewis's image of Christianity as a lens, a way of seeing, a "sun" that illuminates and clarifies reality, I've come to understand that Christianity *is* hyphenated. It's a religion of paradoxes. Of dissonant and seemingly contradictory truths that reveal the roominess of God. Every facet of it—from its theology to its ethics to its holy book to its founder's own identity—is steeped in paradoxes that hold us in wonderful, fertile tension. Its "bridge" is wide and expansive, and if we can find the courage to step onto it, it will make a Way forward for all of us.

Maybe, to switch metaphors, paradox is the key to God's big house.

The paradoxes that characterize this "dissonant way" are so numerous that we could ponder them for lifetimes. I've already touched on some in previous chapters:

God is Three, and God is One.
Jesus is God, and Jesus is human.
God is immanent, and God is transcendent.
The Bible is God's Word, and the Bible is a human
      document.
Creation is good, and creation is broken.
I'm a sinner, and I'm a saint.

Jesus is Lord, and Jesus is a servant.
God's kingdom is here, and God's kingdom is coming.
Death is undone, and death is all around us.
God is just, and God is love.
To give is to receive.
To die is to live.
To forgive is to be forgiven.
To serve is to reign.
The weak are strong.
The foolish are wise.
The persecuted are blessed.
The meek will inherit the earth.
We rest when we bear the yoke.
We live when we shoulder the cross.
We wield power when we surrender.
We possess all things when we keep nothing.

This list is far from exhaustive, but it demonstrates how central paradox is to Christianity. Again and again, the way of Jesus invites us to hold opposing truths together, in pairings that seem impossible. This is not to confound us but to show us how wide and spacious the realm of God really is.

These days, I would go so far as to say that God *prefers* paradox—or, at the very least, that God seems much more comfortable with it than we are. Given a choice between *either* and *or,* the God I see in Scripture sidesteps the binary altogether and chooses *and.* Justice *and* mercy, revelation *and* mystery, now *and* not-yet.

To be clear, I haven't come to this embrace of paradox lightly. I know how hard it is to live with dissonance. I know how alluring an either-or approach to life and faith can be. I spent years trying to scrub my faith clean, smooth, and friction-free.

But I've come to understand that the seeming contradictions that characterize our faith give it heft and credibility. Contradictions mirror the world we actually inhabit: a world of messiness, tension, nuance, and ambiguity. If I live in a world that's full of conflict, if I'm facing challenges that defy easy answers, if I have to spend my days shifting between competing identities, then I need a spiritual tradition that's robust enough to hold all of that complexity.

Okay, but what does it mean to see by the light of paradox? How do we do it? What does such seeing require of us?

It's no coincidence that many of the heresies that have rocked orthodox Christianity over the past two thousand years have grown from an unwillingness to sit patiently with paradox. As in: Jesus *can't* be fully God and fully human, so let's choose one. God *can't* be immanent and transcendent at the same time, so let's go with transcendence. A good God doesn't allow good people to suffer, so I must have done something bad to deserve this misfortune.

It takes courage to say, "Yes, this is true—*and this is true also.* I don't know how, but God does, which means there is an invitation in this dissonance. There is a richness in the tension of this both-and. God is present here. God is roomy here. I can safely inhabit this space."

Seeing by the light of paradox means surrendering the need to *know* once and for all. It means approaching uncertainty with curiosity rather than fear, and training our souls not simply to tolerate but to *savor* the hyphenated realms of our spiritual lives.

There's enough truth to go around. There's no need to jostle and shove, no need to stick our truths in each other's faces, no need to hoard or hide what we discover, keeping ourselves nourished while others starve.

A religion of paradox is not a religion of neat answers. It's a religion of beautiful, thought-provoking questions that are capable of holding joy and sorrow, faith and doubt, knowing and unknowing together. This is why Jesus spent so much of his time asking questions that seemed to stump his listeners: "Who do you say that I am?" "What do you want me to do for you?" "Does this offend you? "Why do you call me good?" "Are you asleep?" "Do you want to get well?" "Do you want to leave, too?" "Why are you afraid?"

Jesus recognized that inhabiting such questions—facing them, carrying them, mulling them over—was essential and generative. He was never in a rush to "close the deal" with the people he met; in fact, he very often allowed them to walk away, pondering whatever it was he'd said to them. The rich young man walked away. Nicodemus (initially) walked away. The disciples who found the idea of eating Jesus's flesh and drinking his blood repulsive walked away. In every case, Jesus let them be.

A religion of paradox—a religion of living, breathing questions—is a patient religion. The church hasn't always honored this fact, but it is true nevertheless. A religion of paradox understands that contradiction is not proof of God's absence; it's proof that God is close. That illumination is near. That truth is at hand. As an unnamed Puritan poet once expressed it in prayer:

Lord, high and holy, meek and lowly,
Thou hast brought me to the valley of vision,
  where I live in the depths but see Thee in the heights;

hemmed in by mountains of sin I behold Thy glory.
Let me learn by paradox that the way down is the way up,
that to be low is to be high,
that the broken heart is the healed heart,
that the contrite spirit is the rejoicing spirit,
that the repenting soul is the victorious soul,
that to have nothing is to possess all,
that to bear the cross is to wear the crown,
that to give is to receive,
that the valley is the place of vision.

The valley of paradox is so much roomier, more colorful, and more textured than the two-dimensional landscapes of faith we often choose. If we're willing to linger in the valley, we'll experience what C. S. Lewis experienced: Christianity as "sun." As vision. As a way of seeing that is sharp and revealing, ample and generous. We won't have to turn our brains off to follow the way of Jesus. We won't have to sidestep every question that eludes an easy or immediate answer. We won't have to stand at the edge of dissonance, quaking in fear. We'll be able to step onto that bridge and find God right there with us, holding our hands, steadying our feet, and beckoning us forward.

Giving all the paradoxes of Christianity their due in a meaningful way would take volumes. In this chapter, I want to highlight just three that have helped me find my way to a more spacious faith.

The first might seem a bit abstract and difficult. Indeed, the paradox of the Holy Trinity—Father, Son, and Holy Spirit, or

Creator, Redeemer, and Sustainer— might be the most mysterious of them all. Christians have found it puzzling for two thousand years. I still remember the earnest and well-meaning Sunday school teachers from my childhood who attempted to explain it: "God is like water! Water exists in three states, right? Liquid, solid, and gas? God is like that! Or like an egg: the shell, the egg white, and the yolk? Three parts, one egg! Or a three-leaf clover! Or a tree: the roots, the trunk, and the branches—but they make up one tree, right? Or, um, a triangle! Three angles, one shape!"

These analogies were vaguely helpful in unpacking the *how* of the Trinity, but they didn't answer the much more pressing question of *why*. As in: Why should we care? Why does the Trinity matter? What does it reveal about who God is and who we, as God's image-bearers, might become?

These have been urgent questions since the earliest years of the faith, but I think they're particularly urgent now, given the divided, fragmented times we live in. Religion is so often used as a weapon of war these days. In our fear, anxiety, and defensiveness, we hunker down with our chosen communities and lob grenades at everyone on the outside. We assume that we have a monopoly when it comes to the Divine. We grow smug and complacent, insisting that *our* articulation of faith, *our* liturgy, *our* denomination, and *our* worship practices capture the best version of who God is and what God desires.

This is where the paradox of the Trinity offers its most incisive challenge. By its very complexity it humbles and awes us, challenging our thoughtless assumptions of superiority. The Trinity says that the truth of God will *always* exceed us. The truth of God will always be more than our tiny, easily overwhelmed minds can bear. The truth of God will always confront, convict, and remake us, even as it soothes and affirms us. This is a good thing. It is good and right and necessary to remember that *we* are created in *God's* image. We are not at liberty to shape God into ours.

In his beautiful and transformative book *The Divine Dance*, Richard Rohr argues that we can't answer the *why* of the triune God unless we start in the right place: "Don't start with the One and try to make it into Three," he writes, "but start with the Three and see that this is the deepest nature of the One."

Start with the Three—what spectacular dissonance for us mono-theists! One of my ongoing struggles as a South Asian American Christian is negotiating between "I" and "we," between indi-vidualism and collectivism. I know how much American culture prizes self-reliance, independence, creativity, privacy, initiative, and boldness. I know how deeply Indian culture values inter-dependence, cooperation, loyalty, conformity, respectfulness, and social harmony.

Most of all, I know how hard it is to inhabit a life-giving space between these two cultures, each of which understands and evaluates personhood so differently.

So for me, the Trinity is both fascinating and useful. *Three* dis-tinct individuals. *One* Godhead. How might this paradox speak to both the cultures I inhabit? What would it look like to, as Rohr suggests, "start with the Three"? What would we discover about God's character, God's personality, and God's priorities if we saw "Threeness" as the very ground and essence of God's being?

If Three is the deepest nature of the One, then God is not rigid or static. Threeness requires fluidity, dynamism, communication, and movement. Or to use Rohr's evocative language again: It describes a God who flows and *is* flow. A God who dances and *is* dance. Each person in the Trinity contributes uniquely to this dance, enhancing it with their particular movements, rhythms, and sensibilities. Their particularity matters. But it's only *in concert* that the Trinity's sacred choreography comes to life.

As I contemplate this image, I think about what it means to follow a dancing God. A God who moves and changes. A God who bridges the individual and the collective in a way that leads to rich, synchronous beauty. I wonder what kinds of flexibility, adaptability, and openness I need to cultivate within myself to emulate such a God.

At the same time, if God is both Three and One, then God is also *diverse*. Each Person— Father, Son, and Holy Spirit—has a unique and individual way of embodying and expressing truth, beauty, love, and justice. This means that *goodness itself* is plural. It is not one thing; it is many things. What would it look like to see goodness as varied and multihued? What kind of humility do I need to foster to receive and affirm the goodness of the other? How can I learn to see the good in cultural practices, traditions, and rituals I don't recognize or understand?

If the Three reflects the deepest nature of the One, then God is not a loner. Even in God's individuality, God is community, relationship, and intimacy. God is *hospitality*. God welcomes, and God is welcomed. God is host, and God is guest. God initiates, and God receives.

In the fifteenth century, Russian iconographer Andrei Rublev created *The Hospitality of Abraham*, also known as *The Trinity*, one of the most well-known and well-loved icons in Christendom. In it, the Father, the Son, and the Holy Spirit, depicted as the three angels who appeared to Abraham near the great trees of Mamre, sit around a table, sharing food and drink.

Their faces are nearly identical, but they're dressed in different colors. The Father wears gold, the Son blue, and the Spirit green. The Father gazes at the Son. The Son gazes back at the Father but gestures toward the Spirit. The Spirit gazes at the Father but points toward the Son with one hand and opens up the circle with the other, making room for others to join the sacred meal.

As a whole, the icon exudes adoration and intimacy—clearly, the three persons around the table love and enjoy each other. But it also exudes openness. There is space at the table for the viewer of the icon. For me. For us. As if to say: the point of the great Three-in-One is not exclusivity but radical hospitality. God is not a middle-school clique. The point of the Three is always to add one more, to extend the invitation, to make the holy table more expansive and more welcoming. In fact, the deeper the intimacy between the Three grows, the roomier the table becomes. The closer we draw to the Three, the wider and more hospitable our own hearts grow toward the world.

And finally, God's Threeness means that the force that holds the universe together—the signature force that resides at the heart of the Godhead and therefore at the heart of all reality—is love. The relationship between the Father, the Son, and the Holy Spirit is not a relationship of domination, manipulation, competition, or jealousy. It's a relationship of compassion, adoration, and deep communion. It's a relationship of the most profound intimacy.

Perhaps this is why St. Paul, writing to the cantankerous Christians in Corinth, insists that love is the greatest of the spiritual virtues. It's when we love that we most closely mirror the heart of God. Like the Trinity, whose imprint we bear, we need to be creatures motivated first and foremost by love. The kind of love that simultaneously honors and transcends difference. The kind of love that celebrates the other above the self.

This begs the question: Is love *my* signature? Is love my motivation, my impetus, my goal, my beating heart? If not, then how do I need to change?

The paradox of the Trinity opens the house of faith very wide. It assures me that I am the child of a huge God: a mysterious, fluid, diverse, communal, hospitable, and intimate God.

We could easily spend the rest of our lives exploring this single paradox—God's Three-in-Oneness—for the wealth of wisdom it offers. How might we live into God's perfect balance of Oneness and Threeness—the individual and the communal? What would it look like to see ourselves as distinct and precious individuals, and at the same time lean into the diversity we see all around us? Where in our lives do we need to expand the table of fellowship and practice the radical interdependence, hospitality, and communion of the triune God?

⁓

A second paradox I've found both healing and illuminating is the paradox of God's power. The paradox of a God whose omnipotence lies in servanthood. The power of a king who washes feet. The power of an Almighty who dies a criminal's death. The power we're called to wield as we take up our crosses and follow Jesus.

I knew about Jesus the Servant King growing up—after all, I read the Jesus-washes-feet story every Maundy Thursday—but somehow he didn't make the lasting impression he needed to make. Maybe he lived too far back in the shadows of the other God—the omnipotent, muscular superhero God I heard about far more often in church.

The hymns I learned and sang so eagerly as a little girl—"All Hail the Power," "I Sing the Mighty Power of God," Praise to the Lord, the Almighty"—were all about this God. The power of this God resided in his ability to unilaterally control people, places, and events. He wielded his strength by flooding the earth, toppling towers, cursing snakes, parting seas, and slaughtering firstborns.

As a child, I watched the adults in my life do all sorts of theological gymnastics to square this God's brand of omnipotence with another equally essential divine trait: goodness. "God allows" is the phrase I heard most often in defense of the all-powerful formula: "Bad things happen because God *allows* them to happen. Nothing happens without God's express foreknowledge and permission. God is perfectly capable of intervening against evil and suffering; when God doesn't, it's only because God has chosen to exercise restraint in order to accomplish some higher purpose."

This "higher purpose" was most often a mystery, though we were free to speculate: Did God allow the hurricane in order to demonstrate God's power over nature? Maybe God allowed the neck injury in order to build character. It's possible the chemotherapy failed because God wanted to take a beloved child home to heaven. Could God have allowed the bomb to explode to punish sin?

It was a neat formula; it seemed to cover all the bases and explain the inexplicable. I believed it for as long as I could. Until I couldn't anymore.

I don't know what the final straw was that wrecked my belief in God as Iron Man. The vindictive, racist sermons I heard after 9/11? A sudden, senseless death in my extended family? The medical conditions that afflicted my own children? All I know is that the supreme power attributed to God by so many Christians began to sound sinister, grievous, and false. I started to wonder if the fantasies of earth-shattering power we impose on God are just that: our own lustful fantasies. Maybe we conjure a super-hero God because we're afraid of vulnerability—our own vulnerability as well as God's. Or maybe we like the way a muscular, thunderous God gives us permission to remain passive and complacent as the world around us groans and trembles.

After all, why bother getting involved in the world's sorrows when everything that happens or doesn't happen is God's will? Why lean into our own creativity, respond to our own deep longings for justice, or call each other out to engage in the slow, risky work of renewing creation when "God's plan" will take care of everything? Why relate to God as someone who longs to be loved, desired, explored, and enjoyed when we can reduce God to a dealmaker, a Superman, or a Santa Claus?

Growing up brown-skinned and female, I learned early on that the power Western culture values is the power of control. The *point* of being powerful is to get your own way. To impose your will on others. To maximize your own gain.

None of this reflects the paradoxical power of the God I see in Scripture. In the pages of the Hebrew Bible, God nurtures, woos, grieves, relents, forgives, and restores humanity again and again. In the Gospels, God enters our world in the lowliest possible way: a sovereign in a stable, a king on a donkey, a Lord on a cross.

I recognize how hard it is to let go of an omnipotent God who promises us safety and security. But the paradox of true divine power is that God chooses vulnerability over security. God's power resides in places we'd never think to look. The soft swell of a pregnant teenager's belly, a tiny mouth drawing nourishment from an aching breast, the mewling cries of a swaddled newborn: these tender moments demonstrate the power of God to enter fully into our world. The great displays of power this incarnate God shows us include riding on a donkey, washing dirty feet, hanging on a cross, and frying fish on a beach for his agnostic friends.

The truth is, a God who would wield power like we do would not be a *good* God. But a good God is precisely what we have in Emmanuel, the God who is with us. The God who weeps, laughs, aches, and celebrates with us is a God who is strong enough to place God's self squarely in the hot center of humanity's pain—not as one who remains safely anesthetized but as one who knows the terrors of human vulnerability from the inside out.

The older I get, the more awe I feel at the power God has to accompany us as creation groans and as we groan along with it. I aspire to this power, but I don't wield it well; I'm tempted to cut and run all the time. One more mass shooting, one more devastating earthquake, one more fatal cancer diagnosis, and I am felled—numb, curled inward, *done.*

What kind of omnipotence enables God to hold all the world's brutality, agony, and sorrow within God's heart and not fold into cynicism or despair? What kind of power fuels such amazing stamina, such risky hope, such healing, life-giving empathy? I don't pretend to know. All I can do is kneel before it, because it's a power that is genuinely good. It's a power that accompanies, sustains, redeems, and resurrects. It's the power of surrender, the power of vulnerability, the power of kenosis. *This is the power we are called to cherish and cultivate.*

———

One last paradox I'm finding helpful these days is a paradox involving time. I call it the paradox of Holy Saturday. It's the paradox of "the now and the not-yet," as in: the kingdom of God is here, *and* the kingdom of God is coming. Jesus is Lord now, *and* evil still holds sway in the world. The grave is already empty, *and* we live in the long shadow of the cross. Good Friday and Easter Sunday are both past. And yet we live on Holy Saturday.

I find this paradox helpful because it teaches me a virtue that doesn't come easily: The virtue of patience. The practice of waiting. Not passive waiting, but active waiting—waiting with joy, bated breath, anticipation.

Many of us live in a culture that worships instant gratification and primes us to expect solutions to all our problems right now. We can order just about anything on Amazon and find it on our doorstep within twenty-four hours. We can send a text, an email, or a Facebook message across the ocean and have it arrive instantaneously. We have 24/7 access to information, health care, nourishment, and shelter. In this cultural economy, delays are considered a waste of precious time. Worse, delays are automatic reasons to doubt the love and goodness of God.

And yet as I look at Scripture, I find that waiting is not only the norm; it's nearly a vocation. The biblical pattern for God's people is a pattern of waiting. Adam waits for a partner, Noah waits for the floodwaters to recede, Abraham and Sarah wait for a son, Jacob waits to marry Rachel, Hannah waits for children, the Israelites wait for deliverance . . . the list goes on and on.

In a broader and more metaphorical sense, waiting is the sacred work of the church. We proclaim the mystery of faith every Sunday morning: "Christ has died. Christ is risen. Christ will come again." We rightfully pin our hopes on that last claim, and yet, in our humanness, we grow weary of waiting. A few years ago, I was in church, sitting in a pew beside a woman in her nineties. Her wheelchair was in the aisle beside her. At one point in the liturgy, she turned to me and whispered, "Two thousand years. And *still* we wait." She wasn't complaining, exactly. But her words were poignant, and I could feel her tiredness in my bones.

What does it mean to wait for what is here and not here at the same time? More importantly, *why* does God want us to wait? I don't have answers, just wonderings. Musings. Hopes. As I struggle to wait, and as I watch others struggle with this apparently universal vocation, here are some of the things I wonder.

I wonder if waiting is the only way I can receive God as God really is. It has taken me years to recognize how my insistence on quick answers to prayer distorts my image of God. If God doesn't give me what I want right when I want it, then I need to ask myself what kind of God I believe in. Can I trust in a God whose generosity and timing look different than I want them to? Or do I believe in a God whose behavior I can reduce to a formula?

Waiting forces me to consider the possibility that God is wilder, less predictable, and less "safe" than my need for immediate comfort dictates. It compels me to look for God in lonelier, more shadowy places, and not merely in the light of answered prayer. Waiting challenges me to rethink the relationship between

God's goodness and my desires. God can say no. God can withhold. God can subject God's self to the limits that come with the created order God has established. And yet God can still be good.

I wonder if waiting is the only way I can learn to accept reality as it is. I tend to be perfectionistic and even combative about my circumstances. It's hard for me to live intentionally and fully in the life I have now; I always want to change a few things first. Tidy up, fix up, and resolve. Richard Rohr writes that forgiveness is central to Jesus's teaching "because to receive reality is always to 'bear it,' to bear with reality for not meeting all of our needs. To accept reality is to forgive reality for being what it is, almost day by day and sometimes even hour by hour. Such a practice creates patient and humble people."

I am the least open to God when I'm demanding the most *from* God. When my heart is clamoring. When the "give me, give me, give me" prayers are pouring out of me at a hundred miles an hour. When I am clenched inside. Unreceptive. Ungenerous. And immature. I am incapable in those moments of hearing how petulant and frantic I sound. I lose all ability to make use of my own God-given resources and strengths. When I'm in demand mode, it doesn't even occur to me to consider what God might want *me* to do. I become willfully helpless, and my thinking loses agency and nuance. Perhaps waiting is the only way I can accept who *I* really am. Waiting forces me to slow down and to stop yammering.

A few years ago, my church organized its annual parish retreat around the theme of "Listening with Love." We were led by a pastor who is also a musician, who talked about music as an apt metaphor for living in community as God's church.

It's hard sometimes, he told us, to listen to other people's music. Our own songs, and song genres, are precious to us; they carry deeply meaningful associations and memories. We have songs we hang onto from our childhoods. Songs we played at our weddings. Songs we use as lullabies for our children. Often, our songs are our most direct lines to God.

Other people's music, on the other hand, can grate on our ears. A jazz lover might not have any patience for country music. If your favorite playlist is chock-full of pop tunes, you might not appreciate opera, or hard rock, or heavy metal. Listening to other people's music can be painful, irritating, or even impossible. That is, it can be impossible if we don't cultivate a practice of curious, generous, sacrificial love.

At one point in his teaching, our presenter had us break into four-part harmony, hold a chord, and then modulate the chord according to his instructions. "Altos, up a half step. Good. Now tenors, down a third. Great! Sopranos, down a step. Basses, up a half." As the chord we were holding became dissonant and strange, we had to strain to listen to each other—to blend our voices not only in terms of pitch but also tone, texture, and volume.

For me, the experience was double-edged. On the one hand, I was intrigued by the dissonance; I wanted to know where it would take us next. On the other, I ached for resolution because the tension was so challenging.

This is the Church of the Dissonant Way. The Church of Holy Paradox. This is how we're called to live as Christ's followers: Walk into the tension and hold it. Listen hard for the notes beneath the notes so that whatever unity we achieve is nuanced and true. Accept dissonance as essential to the songs we create together.

Of course, it's far easier to wax eloquent about dissonance as a spiritual metaphor than it is to listen with love to those who grate on us for any number of good reasons. But then, why did we ever think it would be easy? When Jesus says, "Love your enemies and pray for those who persecute you" (Matthew 5:44), why have I assumed that somehow he's kidding? Or that he's talking to everyone else but me?

The fact is, very little in either my social or religious life these days facilitates radical, dissonance-oriented listening. My friends tend to hold many of the same political opinions I do. The news sources I turn to almost invariably reinforce my perspectives. I worship with people who, by and large, hold the same beliefs I hold. And this problem isn't unique to me; as a whole, American Christians live in safe seclusion from each other's differences.

As I look out over the religious landscape of twenty-first-century America, I wonder what an active, loving dissonance might look like in the church. Beneath the cacophony of sexism, racism, and nationalism, can I discern other notes? Notes of economic desperation? Notes of fear? Notes of alienation? Or on the other hand, beneath the noise of progressive virtue signaling, can I hear chords of pain, yearning, injustice, and loss?

Can I listen with love to the angry song of the laid-off coal miner in West Virginia whose views on immigration might be tied, in part, to his dwindling capacity to feed his family? The song of the pro-life activist whose passion for the unborn child is as genuinely compassion-driven as mine for the incarcerated teenager or the Ukrainian refugee? The song of the conservative pastor who genuinely doesn't see a way to reconcile the authority of the Bible he loves with the sanctity of gay marriage?

Much closer to home: Can I listen to the music of the conservative Indian pastor who shunned me when I wouldn't cover my head in church? The songs of a college friend who walked away when I told her I support marriage equality? The melodies of the atheist who laughs because I believe in the resurrection? The harmonies of the priest who considers my feminism insufficiently feminist?

It still astonishes me to realize that when Jesus commands me to love my neighbors, he actually wants me to love into the dissonance. To love the one who is most unlike me. To love across the hyphens, the barriers, the divides, and the bridges. NPR: love Fox News. Taizé: love praise bands. Marcus Borg: love Rick Warren. Altar calls: love liturgy.

Most of this feels impossible. But maybe that's the greatest paradox of all: that God can accomplish in us what we can't accomplish in ourselves. Left to myself, I will never love as I ought to. That's why I've come to cherish the Way of Dissonance. God is okay with the many *both-ands* I carry around inside of me. God can work in my in-between spaces, creating possibilities that are invisible to me but not to God.

10 | LIMPS AND WORMS: WRESTLING

A few years ago, a close friend sent me a cartoon drawing for Christmas. I keep it on my desk and look at it often. Every time I do, I smile.

It's a drawing of a man and a little girl, facing each other and standing two or three feet apart. The man's arm is extended, and his long fingers are pressed gently against the child's forehead. There's a look of supreme patience, affection, and amusement on his face.

The girl, meanwhile, is fury personified. Her pigtails are flying, her fists and teeth are clenched, and her feet look like they're moving so fast they'll never hit the ground again. She's headed for the man with all the intensity of a bull aimed at a red cape, and though her arms are too short to reach him, it's clear she wants to knock him to the ground. The only thing preventing the headbutt she craves is his restraining hand on her forehead.

"It's you," my friend explained in the note accompanying the Christmas gift. "It's you, fighting God."

My friend knows me so well. This is what I do. I fight with God.

On its face, *wrestling* doesn't sound like a particularly spacious or welcoming metaphor for the spiritual life. What does fighting have to do with roominess, anyway? If it's true that we are living in God's big house, who wants to spend their days here engaging the Divine in active combat?

Plenty of people don't, and that's okay. I know many wonderful Christians—my faithful mother among them—who simply have no need to wrestle. Faith comes gently to them. They don't get stuck on questions about human suffering, or contradictions in the Bible, or Genesis and evolution, or the biology of the virgin birth. They're not shaken and rattled when they can't understand the *hows* and *whys* of Christian doctrine and practice; they're content to let God be God and move on with their lives. In short, they practice their faith in the way the ancient psalmist once described: "I do not occupy myself with things too great and too marvelous for me. But I have calmed and quieted my soul, like a weaned child with its mother; my soul is like the weaned child that is with me" (Psalm 131:1–2).

I envy their spiritual serenity. I really do. And I'm so grateful that it exists as a version of faith; we need its steady witness so much.

But I can't relate to it. I'm a wrestler. I've always been a wrestler, so I have a tender spot in my heart for people who come at God like the little girl in my cartoon: eyes ablaze, fists clenched, sneakered feet hurtling through space to make contact. As it turns out, the house of God has room for sacred combat.

———————

I spent the first many years of my life feeling bad about this aspect of my spiritual life. I thought that my wrestling was a sign of faithlessness. Or rebellion. Or disrespect. Or arrogance. I thought that my questions and objections were offensive to God, so I spent just as much time repenting of my wrestling matches as I did actually wrestling. I believed that if I tried harder, I could eventually tamp down the wildness inside. Use my inside voice, walk on eggshells, please and appease, be a good girl.

I had no idea that God might be okay with my feistiness or that, in fact, God might take delight in it. It never occurred to me to read the great stories of Scripture through the lens of holy combat.

Abraham contends with God over the fate of Sodom and Gomorrah. Moses dukes it out over God's wrath toward the idolatrous Israelites. David pours out his disappointment and fury into psalm after psalm after psalm. Job dares God to show up and answer his bitter questions. What are these stories if not stories of human beings running at God in the full heat of their frustration, bewilderment, sorrow, and alarm?

In the end, two particular stories from Scripture changed my perspective on holy wrestling. Honestly, I don't know if I'd still be a Christian without them.

The first is the story of Jacob's epic wrestling match near the river Jabbok, as recorded in Genesis 32. The story of Jacob the trickster's violent encounter with an unnamed stranger in the night has given me permission to bring my whole turbulent self before God and to engage with the Divine in ways that feel contentious before they become consoling. These days, Jacob's experience fundamentally shapes my view of God. Because of his story, wrestling has become my portal into faith.

As the story begins, Jacob is returning to the place of his birth after twenty years away. He is steeling himself to reunite with Esau, the brother whose life he ruined through deceit and manipulation. Jacob has no idea how Esau will receive him, and he's afraid. After sending his wives, his concubines, his children, and all his possessions ahead across the river, Jacob decides to spend the night alone. Scripture doesn't tell us why, but of course we can speculate. Maybe he wants to pray and beg God for help. Maybe, as is his wont, Jacob wants to scheme and strategize for a while before facing his brother. Maybe he's overwhelmed by anxiety and wishes to hide. Or maybe he's a coward who wants his family to run into Esau first and smooth things over for him.

We don't know. All we know is that Jacob is isolated and vulnerable in a way he hasn't been for a long time. On this lonely night, he can't hide behind his vast wealth, or his many servants, or his large and complicated family, since they're all gone. He is alone in the dark in a desolate place . . . until he's not. A nameless, faceless stranger suddenly leaps out of nowhere and throws him to the ground.

Already, the story resonates with me personally. How often have I found myself alone in the dark in a desolate place? How often, amid those menacing shadows, have I done solitary battle with something I wouldn't recognize as God until much, much later?

Scholars have debated for years about what really happens in the Jacob story. Is he attacked by robbers? Does he have a panic attack? Is the stranger really Esau in disguise? For me, it doesn't matter. It doesn't matter because *all* the epic battles of my life—my battles with guilt, shame, fear, doubt, grief, or unforgiveness; my wrestling matches with family, friends, enemies, community, church, and creed—have ultimately been battles with and about God.

It is with God, and in relationship to God, and in God's all-encompassing presence that we fight the fights that bend, break, and remake us. It is in God's company that we face down the demons within and around us. God alone brings us to the ragged edges of our own strength so that finally, *finally*, we'll surrender and allow ourselves to be saved. Whether we recognize the stranger as God or not, God is always the one we're really struggling with when the fight feels existential, urgent, and larger than life. God is always the one who battles us—not for our detriment but for our transformation.

Jacob and "the man" wrestle, the text says, all night long. They wrestle until Jacob is almost sure he will prevail. They wrestle, their limbs entangled and their eyes fixed on each other, until the darkness breaks and they see the dawn.

Here again, the story speaks to me powerfully. I was six or seven years old when I first learned Jacob's story in Sunday school, and it terrified me. A violent man leaping out of the darkness? A pitched battle that lasted for hours? God, in the guise of an angel or a man or a demon or a *something*, dislocating Jacob's hip and abandoning him by a river? The whole narrative struck me as ominous, the stuff of horror movies and nightmares. What kind of God did such creepy things? Wasn't God supposed to be loving? Protective? Safe?

The God who goes toe-to-toe with Jacob is not a God whose first priority is our ease and comfort. Jacob's God is not a God who maintains a polite distance, minds God's manners, or "makes nice" to keep us happy. No. Jacob's God is wild and mysterious, unpredictable and strange. Jacob's God doesn't hesitate to muck around in the mud for several hours to bring Jacob to his knees. Indeed, the Hebrew word for *wrestle* means "to get dusty." To get dirty. This is no dainty, breakable God. This is a God of dust and sweat and blood and tears—a God who is willing to become dirty to lift us out of the dirt.

As I've already written, Jacob's God is not the God I grew up with. As a child and a teenager, I thought of God as terribly fragile. Easily offended, easily upset, easily put off. My job as a good Christian girl was to obey the rules and keep this delicate Divinity happy at all costs. One false turn, one impertinent question, or one sullied bit of doctrine, and that fine teacup of a God might get knocked off the table and shatter.

What a contrast to the God who spends an entire night by a muddy river, duking it out with a human. This is a God who wants to engage. A God we can throw ourselves against with the full weight of our thoughts, questions, ideas, and feelings. A God who invites our rigor, our persistence, our intensity, and our strength. This is a God who doesn't let go.

As the night wears on and the stranger sees that Jacob has no intention of giving up, he strikes Jacob on the hip socket, dislocating his hip and causing him to limp. In "The Magnificent Defeat," a beautiful sermon on this story, Frederick Buechner describes the pivotal moment like this:

All the night through they struggle in silence until just before morning, when it looks as though a miracle might happen. Jacob is winning. The stranger cries out to be set free before the sun rises. Then, suddenly, all is reversed.

He merely touches the hollow of Jacob's thigh, and in a moment Jacob is lying there crippled and helpless. The sense we have, which Jacob must have had, that the whole battle was from the beginning fated to end this way, that the stranger had simply held back until now, letting Jacob exert all his strength and almost win so that when he was defeated, he would know that he was truly

defeated; so that he would know that not all the shrewd-
ness, will, brute force that he could muster were enough
to get this. Jacob will not release his grip, only now it
is a grip not of violence but of need, like the grip of a
drowning man.

We live in a culture that celebrates success and scorns defeat.
But sometimes defeat is a mercy. Defeat is what saves us. What I
carry away from the story of Jacob's wounding is the troubling
but rock-solid truth that blessing and bruising are not mutually
exclusive in the realm of God. We can limp and prevail at the
same time. We can experience healing in brokenness. If I want
to engage with God, then I must expect that I will be changed
in the process—and not always in ways that are painless or comfortable or easy. I can't dictate the terms of blessing. I can't say
I want the blessing but not the limp. Sometimes the blessing *is*
the limp.

As dawn breaks, the stranger asks Jacob to disengage, and
Jacob, tenacious as ever, says no: "I will not let you go, unless you
bless me" (Genesis 32:26). I love this line. I adore it. I want to make
it my life's mantra, because it assures me that sometimes "winning" involves nothing more sophisticated than not giving up.
Sometimes the spiritual life is about little more than encounter-
ing a God who feels mysterious, nameless, opaque, bewildering,
and frightening and then hanging on for dear life. Sometimes the
whole of Christianity comes down to saying, "There's so much I
can't wrap my head around, but I know that there's a blessing in
this mess somewhere. I will hang on until I find it."

So Jacob hangs on, waiting for something good to happen,
and the stranger consents to his request for a blessing. But first, he

asks Jacob the terrible but essential question upon which the blessing is predicated: "What is your name?"

Why is that question terrible? Because Jacob has some painful history with this question. The first time he heard it, he was twenty years younger and standing in his aging father Isaac's tent, wearing his brother's clothes.

Isaac, wary and suspicious and unable to see, was afraid. He sensed . . . *something.* He knew the immense power of blessing, and he didn't want to make the catastrophic mistake of bestowing it on the wrong person. So he asked once again who was standing in his tent. And young Jacob—trickster Jacob; manipulative Jacob; deceitful, selfish Jacob, whose very name means "heel-grabber" or "go-getter"—looked into his father's failing eyes and lied. "I am Esau, your firstborn" (Genesis 27:19).

Twenty years later, the heel-grabber gets a do-over. Still groaning in pain, he hears the exact same question leave the stranger's lips: "What is your name?" What is your identity? Who are you?

I wonder if this is a question God asks us, too, each time we begin to wrestle—not because God doesn't know who we are but because so often *we* don't. Or we do, but we don't want to face what we know. What is your name? Who are you? No, who are you, *really?* At your core?

What Jacob learns that night by the river is that the big, terrible, life-changing questions we dodge and skirt and evade and ignore return to us again and again and again until we find the courage to look them in the eye and answer them honestly. I'm pretty sure that if Jacob had lied to the stranger yet again, the battle would have continued for another day and night. Or maybe for many days and nights. God would have challenged

Jacob's destructive self-deceptions over and over again until he finally surrendered to the uncomfortable truth: "I am Jacob. The heel-grabber. The deceiver. The schemer. The trickster. I am the man who lied to my father, cheated my brother, manipulated my father-in-law, and abandoned every disaster I created. I am Jacob."

It's only when we name the worst that we can relinquish it. It's only when we confess the ugliness within and around us that God begins the holy work of transformation.

"You shall no longer be called Jacob," the stranger tells his weary opponent. "You shall be called Israel, for you have striven with God and with humans, and have prevailed" (Genesis 32:28).

I can't speak for anyone else, but this moment in the story makes me cringe and laugh at the same time. This is the blessing Jacob receives? *This*? A new name that essentially guarantees him a lifetime of holy struggle? "You shall be called Israel," the stranger says. The name literally means "one who contends with God." I wonder if Jacob hears God chuckle. As in: Say goodbye to the Trickster, Jacob. From here on out, you will be the Wrestler.

Laughing aside, though: What sort of blessing is that?

Not a bad one, actually—not a bad one at all. Wrestling, as it turns out, is not an irreverent thing, because it's the opposite of apathy, the opposite of resignation, the opposite of quitting, the opposite of complacency. It's even the opposite of loneliness. To fight is to stay close, to keep my arms wrapped tight around my opponent. Fighting means I haven't walked away—and God hasn't, either. It means I'm still careening toward my holy opponent at a hundred miles an hour, fists at the ready. It means we both have skin left in the game.

This is both a challenge and an invitation to those of us who think our relationship with God has to be smooth and pretty all the time. It doesn't. The God of Jacob delights in those who strive. The opposite of loving God isn't fighting God. The opposite of loving God is not giving enough of a damn to fight.

I don't worry anymore about wrestling, mine or anyone else's. Wrestling is our best protection against spiritual apathy. Wrestling keeps God relevant in our lives; it keeps God personal. It makes sure that God remains a force to reckon with rather than a dusty relic we stick on a shelf.

Here's another way to think about it: In my human relationships, I don't bother getting worked up when I don't care. I don't fight with people I'm passionless about. To wrestle with God is to insist that God matters.

As the story continues, the sun comes up, and it becomes Jacob's turn to rename the place of his wounding. He calls the muddy wrestling ring "Peniel," saying, "I have seen God face to face, and yet my life is preserved" (v. 30).

It's important to remember and to name the places where God shows up and contends with us. These are holy places, where we lose and find our true names as Mystery wrestles us toward salvation. These are the places where we exhaust our own strength and finally collapse into God's.

Every time we brave these places that leave us blessed and limping all at once, God responds with passionate delight, because God longs to meet us—even when we're bent on bowling God over.

It's in the wrestling ring that the sun rises on our new names. It's in the heat of combat that our aching limbs testify to joy.

Jonah is the reluctant evangelist who spent a few miserable days inside a fish. As odd as his story is, it also keeps me in the Christian fold, contending with God.

The more famous half of Jonah's story is the dramatic first half—the one in which he receives instructions from God to preach to the Ninevites, flees on a ship going the opposite direction, gets thrown overboard, and lands in the belly of a giant fish for three days and three nights.

But my favorite part is actually the second half. Following his preposterous marine adventure, Jonah grudgingly obeys God's instructions and warns the people of Nineveh that their wickedness is about to be punished. But then the impossible happens.

The Ninevites listen to Jonah's warning, take it seriously, and repent. And God, seeing their penitence, changes God's mind and shows them mercy. In other words, Jonah preaches a sermon, and his congregation responds to it! It's every pastor's dream, and you'd think that Jonah would be thrilled. But no. He's furious, and he tells God so in the most animated language he can think of: "Take away my life, for it is better for me to die than to live" (Jonah 4:3). He then hunkers down east of the city, hoping God will change God's mind again and burn Nineveh to the ground.

Instead, God offers Jonah an object lesson using a bush, a worm, and the wind, and then God concludes the lesson with a zinger of a question: "Is it right for you to be angry?" (v. 9).

The question is a fraught one, given the context, because Nineveh isn't just any old city. It is the capital city of Assyria, Israel's bitter enemy. Notorious throughout the ancient Near

East for its violence and depravity, Assyria is the empire that will eventually obliterate the northern kingdom of Israel. To Jonah, then, God's question is a ridiculous one. *Of course* he has a right to be angry. Isn't it right to be angry that God's mercy extends to killers? Isn't it right to be angry when people who break the rules don't get the comeuppance they deserve? Isn't it right to be angry about a grace so reckless and wasteful that it challenges our most cherished assumptions about justice?

God doesn't scold Jonah for his anger. Instead, God engages it with compassion. God even goads it in a playful attempt to broaden Jonah's horizons. God wants the grumpy preacher to see the Ninevites as God sees them. For while the Assyrians are everything Jonah believes them to be—violent, depraved, and wicked—they are also more. They are a "great city," God says, but they "don't know their right hand from their left" (v. 11). In other words, they're human beings made in God's image, but they're lost and broken. What they *deserve* is neither here nor there. What they *need* is compassion.

Theologian and mystic Richard Rohr argues that while many people nowadays associate the word *justice* with retribution and the penal system, Jesus and the prophets clearly practiced something else. We'd now call it "restorative justice." "Jesus never punished anybody," Rohr writes. "He undercut the basis for all violent, exclusionary, and punitive behavior. He became the forgiving victim so we would stop creating victims. . . . Punishment relies on enforcement and compliance but it does not change the soul or the heart. Jesus always held out for the heart."

God challenges Jonah to consider the hard truth that even his worst enemies are God's beloved children. Just as the whale, the bush, the worm, and the wind in Jonah's story belong to

God, so do the Assyrians themselves. They are ultimately God's creations: God's to plant, God's to tend, and God's to uproot. Should God not care for God's own? Is it right for Jonah to be angry?

The story wisely ends with these questions unanswered. We're left with Jonah still sulking, still struggling, still wrestling with God's scandalous compassion and mercy toward Jonah's sworn enemies. As the story closes, Jonah is still outside the city, waiting to see what will happen to the people he hates and God loves.

All too often, we are also left to wrestle with the scandalous goodness of God, a goodness that calls us to become instruments of grace even to those who offend us most deeply. God's goodness gently probes beneath our pieties and asks why we often prefer vindication to rehabilitation—prison cells and death sentences to hospitality and compassion. It exposes our smallness and stinginess, our reluctance to embrace the radical kinship God calls us to embrace. Why do we grab at the second chances God gives us, even as we deny those second chances to others? God's goodness dares us to do the braver and riskier thing: to hold out for the hearts of those who belong to God, whether we like them or not.

Do we have a right to be angry? God knows that the only way to answer this question, and so many others like it, is to wrestle it to the ground. God meets us in the ring, openhanded, willing, forbearing. God's hand rests on us in love, even as we prepare to attack. God's patient love enfolds us, absorbing our anger into God's all-sufficient self. And when we're finally ready, God teaches us our new names.

EPILOGUE: STAYING

In the end, what makes a home truly welcoming is the host who answers the door when we knock, who immediately lifts our weary spirits with a warm smile and a hearty "Come on in!" It's the kind soul who takes our coats, shows us into the living room, and hands us piping mugs of tea as we sit by the fireplace, warming our cold hands. It's the owners of the house who decide to throw its doors wide open so that every tired traveler for miles around can see its beckoning light.

Psalm 23, one of the most familiar psalms in the Bible, describes a God who is an exquisite host. The God of this psalm believes in abundance—we will lack nothing once we enter her house. This God invites us to rest our weary bodies in his fragrant green pastures. This God leads us to cool springs of water when we're parched and thirsty. This God offers us guidance and protection in treacherous places. This God invites us into the dining room and prepares a lavish table for us. This God anoints our heads with oil.

Every time I read this psalm, I think of the women in my life, past and present, who have welcomed me home over the years. My grandmothers in Kerala who held lanterns aloft in the night, cooked breakfasts that made my mouth water, and drew cool water from the well for my baths. My mother, who massaged my aching back, shoulders, and feet with fragrant oils for fifty days in a row both times I gave birth. My mother-in-law, ninety years old now, who lives in Kolkata and prays for her children, her children's spouses, and her grandchildren more faithfully and fervently than anyone else I know. The friends, teachers, and mentors who have stepped into my life as maternal figures over the years, sharing their wisdom, wiping my tears, and making me laugh when I didn't think laughter was possible.

I've found my way into God's roomy house in large part because of these people who have loved me. I've learned to experience God as a generous host because God's good people have walked steadily beside me on my dissonant, hyphenated path.

Like the psalmist, I have discovered a God who sets a table laden with delicious food. She hovers over fragrant, steaming pots in her wrinkly apron. She folds napkins, bakes bread, and pours wine. When the meal is over, this God pours warm, fragrant oil down my hair and over my face, and massages its goodness into my scalp, my shoulders, my back, my feet. When the sun sets, this God leads me to places of deep rest and keeps steady watch over me as I sleep.

Psalm 23 ends with a final, ultimate homecoming—the homecoming that St. Thomas, my ancestors, and all of God's children over the millennia have discovered for themselves: "Surely goodness and mercy shall follow me all the days of my life, and I shall dwell in the house of the Lord forever" (v. 6).

In the end, the roominess of God is an invitation. It's an invitation *to stay.* The choice is entirely ours, of course; we can come and go as we please, and even the choosing itself requires a brave capaciousness on our parts. It might entail changing churches, or seeking new faith expressions, or embracing new spiritual communities. Staying includes wandering and wrestling. It includes learning the ways of lostness in the patient company of God.

The decision—the decision to settle once and for all into the roominess of God—is a decision that's personal and unique for each one of us. No one can explain anyone else's reasons for going or staying.

For the reasons I've outlined in these chapters, I've chosen to stay. Back in 2016, in the throes of struggling with my faith, I wrote a prayer in the form of a prose poem, trying to articulate in a concise way what God's roominess means to me. I titled it "Why I Stay." Over the years the poem has evolved, just as my reasons have. I expect they'll keep evolving for as long as I live. But I want to close this book about the many rooms in God's house with the version of the poem that feels true now, here, today. My prayer is that it will open the doors of the house a bit wider for you, too.

Here is why I stay.

———

Because A was for Adam, B for Bethlehem, and C for Cross, and my first classroom was a pew. Because I played hide-and-seek in the font when the preacher wasn't looking, answered every altar call with a sprint down the aisle, and snuck the leftover communion juice from the glasses the church ladies washed on Mondays. I was hoping—I see this now—to steal another drop of You.

Because decades later I'm still felled by stained glass; by musty old Bibles in patient sanctuaries; by altar cloths, choir robes, and candlewax. Because my breathing slows in your house, my muscles unclench, and I remember how to sing loud and clear. Because You are my rootedness, my air, my water. The dark and frozen ground in which I wait to crack open, die, and blossom. You are the closest I will ever come to flourishing.

Because I love stories and I cherish the ones in your book. Because I'm Eve, and the apple makes sense. I'm Sarah, and my barrenness hurts. I'm Rachel, and I won't surrender my sacred objects. I'm Leah, and I long to be loved. I'm Hagar, and I need to name You in the desert. I'm Miriam, and I'm ever watchful. I'm Mary with the jar, who weeps at your feet. I'm the Magdalene, and I bear witness at tombs. I'm Junia, and my story aches to be told.

Because childhood ends, but childhood hungers do not. Because my first house, first Father, first Mother, first love, first hate, first heartbreak, first safety, first terror, was You.

Because the psalmist got it right: I was cast on you from birth.

Because Peter got it even better: Lord, if I leave, to whom will I go?

Because sorrow has come too many times, and there had better be an afterword to explain it. Because I've stood at gravesides and raged. Because my children have suffered and You have watched. Because bodies failed, minds cracked, hearts broke, and we didn't live happily ever after like the fairy tales promised. Because "on earth as it is in heaven" is all I've got, and if it's not enough, then I am lost. Because "Death, where is thy sting?" feels like a mockery but "Jesus wept" does not.

Because joy comes, too, though it doesn't look anything like it should. Because sometimes—too rarely, but I'll take what I can get—the veil parts, the ground gives way, the skies open, and my hunger for you breaks into the purest communion. The hunger I carry becomes You, incarnate and shining.

Because I know You in the liturgy, in the Word, in the broken bread and spilled wine. I know You in the ancient redwood trees, the winding mountain trails, the shifting edges of the ocean. I hear You in the stillness of the forest, the cacophony of birdsong. I feel You in the gentle embrace of the people I love—their hands your hands, their eyes your eyes, their voices soft echoes of yours.

Because in those moments, the possibility of You grows and grows until I am unhoused and undone, too alive for this world. Because You are my Everlasting Almost—almost here, almost certain, almost always, almost irrefutable. You are the tenuous edge I will live and die on. Because the Almost of You— heartbreaking as it is—is sweeter than any guarantee I will find in this world.

Because You are not who I thought You were, so I must wait for revelation. Because I need someone to wrestle, and You meet me at the river. Because this is no ordinary hunger, and Your manna alone will suffice. Because I will drown unless You part this water. Because the world is dark, but it shimmers at its edges.

Because I'm wild inside, and You are not a tame lion. Because You suffered, and only a suffering God can help. Because my ache for You is the beating heart of my aliveness.

Because I am still your stubborn child and I insist on resurrection.

ACKNOWLEDGMENTS

My deepest gratitude to:

Valerie Weaver-Zercher, my kind and brilliant editor, and to everyone at Broadleaf Books who labored so generously to produce this book.

My creative-writing professors at The Ohio State University, who wisely discerned that I need to write memoir and taught me how.

The beloved communities of faith—past and present—that held doors open for me as I made my winding way into God's roomy house: The Cambridge First Church of the Nazarene, Tremont Temple Baptist Church, The Kerala Christian Fellowship, and St. Mark's Episcopal Church, Palo Alto.

My ancestors of many, many generations, and in particular the remarkable women I come from, who prayed my faith into being and sustain it still.

Alex, Priya, and Kiran, who patiently endure my writing and teach me, by astonishing example, how to love.

NOTES

INTRODUCTION

"Meanwhile, the ranks": "Modeling the Future of Religion in America," Pew Research Center, September 13, 2022, https://www.pewresearch.org/religion/2022/09/13/modeling-the-future-of-religion-in-america/.

"The world for which you have been": Walter Brueggemann, quoted in Isaac Anderson, "A Conversation with Barbara Brown Taylor," *Image Journal,* no. 97, https://imagejournal.org/article/a-conversation-with-barbara-brown-taylor/.

"Disillusionment is, literally": Barbara Brown Taylor, *God in Pain: Teaching Sermons on Suffering* (Nashville: Abingdon, 1998), 20.

CHAPTER 1

"Origin stories are rarely": Rachel Held Evans, *Inspired: Slaying Giants, Walking on Water, and Loving the Bible Again* (Nashville: Nelson, 2018), 9.

"Spiritual maturation requires": Evans, *Inspired,* 17.

"According to The Acts of Thomas": M. R. James, trans., *The Apocryphal New Testament* (Oxford: Clarendon, 1924), http://gnosis.org/library/actthom.htm.

CHAPTER 2

"jerked clean out of the habitual": Thomas Merton, *The Asian Journal of Thomas Merton* (Cambridge, MA: New Directions, 1975), 233.

CHAPTER 3

"There are many variations": Barbara Brown Taylor, *An Altar in the World: A Geography of Faith* (New York: HarperOne, 2009), 83.

"To live in the world as a pilgrim": Chris Armstrong, "Pilgrimage and the Christian Life: A Lenten Meditation," *Public Discourse*, March 5, 2019, https://www.thepublicdiscourse.com/2019/03/49915/.

CHAPTER 4

"In her book": Diana Butler Bass, *Christianity after Religion: The End of Church and the Birth of a New Spiritual Awakening* (New York: HarperOne, 2013), 117.

"God isn't above the fray": Daniel Kirk, "Understanding the Human Jesus," *The Bible for Normal People*, ep. 9, https://tinyurl.com/mr2uer8m.

"the meaning we give to what happens": Barbara Brown Taylor, *An Altar in the World: A Geography of Faith* (New York: HarperOne, 2009), 182.

"In Still": Lauren Winner, *Still: Notes on a Mid-Faith Crisis* (New York: HarperOne, 2013), 172.

"Holocaust survivor": Elie Wiesel, *The Gates of the Forest* (New York: Shocken Books, 1995).

CHAPTER 5

"In a 2009 TED Talk": Chimamanda Ngozi Adichie, "The Danger of a Single Story," *TED*, 2009, https://tinyurl.com/3tndx8rv.

CHAPTER 6

***"In his thought-provoking book"*:** Willie James Jennings, *The Christian Imagination: Theology and the Origins of Race* (New Haven: Yale University Press, 2011).

***"In his exhaustive historical study"*:** Charles Taylor, *A Secular Age* (Cambridge: Harvard University Press, 2018).

***"I'd love to have a Christianity"*:** Richard Beck, *Reviving Old Scratch: Demons and the Devil for Doubters and the Disenchanted* (Minneapolis: Fortress, 2016), 10.

***"Abandoning the language of sin"*:** Barbara Brown Taylor, *Speaking of Sin: The Lost Language of Salvation* (London: Cowley, 2000), 13.

***"No one is climbing"*:** Nadia Bolz-Weber, *Pastrix: The Cranky, Beautiful Faith of a Sinner Saint* (Nashville: Jericho, 2013), 49.

CHAPTER 7

***"I am most disillusioned"*:** Cole Arthur Riley, *This Here Flesh* (New York: Convergent, 2022), 98.

***"the two primary sins"*:** Francis Weller, *The Wild Edge of Sorrow: Rituals of Renewal and the Sacred Work of Grief* (Berkeley: North Atlantic, 2015), xx.

***"It astonishes me"*:** Ross Gay, *The Book of Delights* (Chapel Hill: Algonquin, 2022), 49.

CHAPTER 8

***"In* Wearing God"*:** Lauren Winner, *Wearing God: Clothing, Laughter, Fire, and Other Overlooked Ways of Meeting God* (New York: HarperOne, 2015).

***"As feminist theologian"*:** Mary Daly, *Beyond God the Father* (Boston: Beacon, 1985), 19.

***"In God, in her Fatherhood"*:** Sara Maitland, *A Big-Enough God: A Feminist's Search for a Joyful Theology* (New York: Henry Holt, 1995), 23–24.

"The Gospel is only good news": Michael Fitzpatrick, "For the Meek of the Earth; The Second Sunday in Advent," *Journey with Jesus: A Weekly Webzine for the Global Church,* November 27, 2022, https://www.journeywithjesus.net/essays/3507-for-the-meek-of-the-earth.

"The model came out": Amy Frykholm, *See Me Naked: Stories of Sexual Exile in American Christianity* (Boston: Beacon, 2012), 75.

"Whether you are sick or well": Barbara Brown Taylor, *An Altar in the World: A Geography of Faith* (New York: HarperOne, 2009), 38.

CHAPTER 9

"I believe in Christianity": C. S. Lewis, "They Asked for a Paper," in *Is Theology Poetry?* (London: Geoffrey Bless, 1962), 164–65.

"Lord, high and holy": "The Valley of Vision," in *The Valley of Vision: A Collection of Puritan Prayers and Devotions*, ed. Arthur Bennett (London: The Banner of Truth Trust: 1975), xv.

"Don't start with the One": Richard Rohr, *The Divine Dance: The Trinity and Your Transformation* (New Kensington: Whitaker House, 2016).

"because to receive reality": Richard Rohr, "Forgiving Reality for Being What It Is," From Daily Meditations, Center for Action and Contemplation (https://cac.org/daily-meditations/forgiving-reality-for-being-what-it-is-2017-08-30/).

CHAPTER 10

"All the night through they struggle": Frederick Buechner, *Secrets in the Dark: A Life in Sermons* (New York: HarperOne, 2006), 7.

"Jesus never punished anybody": Richard Rohr, "An Alternative Story." *Daily Meditations*, Center for Action and Contemplation, February 4, 2019, https://cac.org/daily-meditations/an-alternative-story-2019-02-04/.